A RAJNEESH READER

The Great Challenge

OTHER WORKS BY BHAGWAN SHREE RAJNEESH

Published by Grove Press

Hammer on the Rock

My Way: The Way of the White Clouds

A RAJNEESH READER

The Great Challenge

BY BHAGWAN SHREE RAJNEESH

Grove Press, Inc./New York

Copyright © 1982 Rajneesh Foundation International

All Rights Reserved

No part of this book may be reproduced, stored in a retrieval system,
or transmitted in any form, by any means, electronic, mechanical,
photocopying, recording, or otherwise, without the prior written per-
mission of the publisher.

First Evergreen Edition 1982
First Printing 1982
ISBN: 0-394-17934-X
Library of Congress Catalog Card Number: 81-47642

Library of Congress Cataloging in Publication Data

Rajaneesh, Acharya, 1931—
    The great challenge.

    (Grove Press Eastern philosophy and literature
series)
    1. Spiritual life. I. Title. II. Series.
BL624.R3313   299′.93   81-47642
ISBN 0-394-17934-X (pbk.)   AACR2

Manufactured in the United States of America

GROVE PRESS, INC., 196 West Houston Street, New York, N.Y. 10014

Grove Press Eastern Philosophy and Literature Series

Edited by Hannelore Rosset

✳

INTRODUCTION

The Great Challenge of Bhagwan Shree Rajneesh is not just a challenge, it is also an invitation.

In these pages you will find the experience of an enlightened man, of a twentieth century Buddha, as he responds to questions from people like you, from people who sense—as you must, otherwise you would not be reading this book—that there is more to life than meets the eye.

In these pages he deals with it all—from God and faith to existence and consciousness, from frustration and suffering to love and compassion, from life before birth to life after death, from drugs and hypnosis to yoga and meditation, from the miracles of Jesus to the materializations of Sai Baba. It's all here: all fresh, all first-hand.

And if, reading his words, you find a thirst arising in you for the same experience, you have heard his invitation.

George Gurdjieff used to tell his disciples to read his books three times, that it took at least three readings for his words to penetrate. I'll be more compassionate and only suggest three readings of Chapters 1 and 2, the chapters in which Bhagwan speaks in detail about his "jet method," the revolutionary Dynamic Meditation. And this is the crux of his invitation: to try it once and to do it totally is to take the first step toward your own transformation, toward your own Buddhahood.

Try it. It's done at Rajneesh Meditation Centers around

the world. And it's done every day at the Shree Rajneesh Ashram in Poona, where Bhagwan himself is.

Try it. This is the great challenge of Bhagwan Shree Rajneesh.

Swami Krishna Prem
November, 1979

✳

Contents

O N E

Flight of the Alone to the Alone

Please explain what you mean by yoga, the yogi, and meditation.

The first thing to be remembered about meditation is that it is not something that can be done.

Throughout the world people have the notion that meditation means doing something. It is not a doing, it is not an act, it is something that happens. It is not that *you* go to it; *it* comes to you and penetrates you. It destroys you in one way and recreates you in another. It is something so vital and so infinite that it cannot be a part of your doing.

Then what is to be done? You can only create the situation in which it happens. All that you can do is to be vulnerable and open to existence from all sides.

Ordinarily we are like prisons: we are closed up within ourselves with no openings. In a way we are dead. One can say we have become "life-proof": life cannot come to us. We have created barriers and hindrances to life, because life can be dangerous, uncontrollable; it is something which is not in our hands. We have created a closed existence for ourselves so that we can be certain and secure, so that we can be comfortable. This closed existence is convenient, but at the same time it is deadening. The more closed we become, the less alive we are. The more open we become, the more alive we are.

Meditation is an openness to all dimensions, an openness to everything. But to be open to everything is dangerous, to be open to everything unconditionally makes us insecure. It cannot be comfortable because anything can happen. A mind which longs for security, which longs for comfort, which longs for certainty, cannot be a meditative mind. Only a mind which is open to anything that life offers, welcoming each and every thing that happens, even death, can create a situation in which meditation happens.

So the only thing that can be done by you is to be receptive to meditation, to be totally receptive—not to any particular happening but to anything that comes.

Meditation is not a particular dimension, it is a dimensionless existence, an existence that is open to each and every dimension without any conditions, without any longings, without any expectations. If there are any expectations, then the opening will not be total. If there are any conditions, any longings, if there are any "ifs," then the opening cannot be total. No part of you should remain closed. If you are not totally open, then no vital, vigorous, infinite happening can be received by you. It cannot become the guest, and you cannot become the host.

Meditation is just the creation of a receptive situation in which something can happen, and all you can do is wait for it.

A mind that waits is waiting for the unknown, because what is going to happen cannot be known beforehand; you cannot even conceive of it. You may have heard something about it, but that is not *your* knowledge; it remains unknown. A mind that is waiting for the unknown is a mind that is meditative.

When you are waiting for the unknown your knowledge becomes a barrier, because the more aware you are of your knowledge the more solidly you imprison yourself. You must not be in a "knowing" mood, you must be completely ignorant; only then can the unknown come to you. The moment your ignorance becomes aware of itself, the moment you know that you *don't* know, that is the moment you begin to wait for the unknown.

There are two types of ignorant people. The first type are not aware of their ignorance—they automatically think that they know. This is ignorant knowledge. The other type are those who are aware of their ignorance. This is a knowing ignorance. And the moment you become aware of your ignorance you come to the point where knowing begins.

A pundit, a person who thinks he knows, can never be a religious man. A person who thinks that he knows is bound to be non-religious, because the knowledgeable ego is the most subtle thing. But the moment you know your ignorance there is no ego, there is no space in which the ego can exist. The greatest attack on the ego is to become aware of your ignorance; the greatest strengthening of your ego is to claim knowledge.

The second thing that I would like to say about meditation is that your mind must be totally aware of its ignorance. And you can only become aware of your ignorance when your accumulated, borrowed knowledge is known as not-knowledge. It is not knowledge, it is simply information, and information is not knowledge even though that is the way it appears.

A person who knows is not dogmatic about his knowledge; he hesitates. But a person who *thinks* that he knows is dogmatic, assertive; he is absolutely certain.

You must become aware of the fact that what *you* have not known cannot be your knowledge. You cannot borrow knowledge: that is the difference between a theological mind and a religious mind. Theology is one of the most irreligious things in the world and theologians are the most irreligious people, because what has been claimed by them as knowledge is borrowed.

Knowledge never makes any claims, because inherent in it is the phenomenon that the moment one knows, the I is lost. The moment one knows, the ego is no longer there. Knowledge comes when the ego is not, so the ego cannot claim to have it. The ego can only collect information; it can accumulate many facts, it can quote scriptures.

To go into meditation is to transcend your accumulated knowledge. The moment this knowledge is transcended, learning begins. And a learner is something quite different: he never claims that he knows, he is always aware of his ignorance. And the more aware of it he is, the more receptive he becomes to the new.

The moment you have learned something discard it, otherwise there is every possibility that it will become part of your knowing, part of your accumulation. If your knowledge comes from your past experiences, then, too, it is borrowed, because you are not the same person any more. And whether your knowledge is borrowed from the past or it is borrowed from someone else makes no difference at all.

Yesterday's me is far away; it is already dead—it is nowhere to be found except in my memory. Yesterday's me is as "other" to me now as you are. In fact, it is even more "other," because you are nearer to me in time. In this moment, if you can be silent, you *are* me, part and parcel of me.

If I am telling you something that came to me yesterday, it is not *I* who will be talking to you: I will be a dead person, a dead record. I will not be living in this moment, adjusted to this moment. Something that is dead will be asserted through me. And to rely upon something that is dead—it is impossible.

If I am still living in the memory of yesterday, then I am not capable of living today. If I can live yesterday's moments yesterday, then I must live what is happening today this very moment and what I say must come through the me of this moment. If it comes from the dead past, it is borrowed. Even if it comes from me, from my own past, it is dead weight, it is not *knowing*.

Knowing is always spontaneous, whereas all claims are always to past knowledge, to memory. When you borrow from your memory you are not in the moment of knowing. One must not borrow from anyone, not even from one's own past.

One must live moment to moment, and live in such a way that everything which comes to you becomes part of your knowing.

If I look at you, my look can be knowing only if my memory is not in between. If I am looking at you through my memory of our past meetings then I am not really looking at you. But if I can look at you without any burden of the past, the look becomes meditative. If I can touch you without the burden of any experience that my hand has known in the past, the touch becomes meditative. Everything that is innocently spontaneous becomes meditative.

The third point that I would like to stress is that a meditative mind lives moment to moment. It does not accumulate, it lives each moment as it comes. It never goes beyond the here and now, it is always in the now, receptive to each moment as it comes.

What is dead is dead; what has passed is past. The past has gone and the future has not yet come. This moment between the past and the future is the only thing that exists.

The past is part of memory and the future is part of longing. Both are mental; they have no existence in themselves, they are human creations. If mankind did not exist on the earth there would be no past and no future. There would just be the present, the now, only *now*—without any passage of time, without any coming, any going. The meditative mind lives in the now—that is its only existence.

A Zen monk was sentenced to death. The king of the country called him and said to him, "You have only twenty-four hours—how are you going to live them?"

The monk laughed and said, "Moment to moment—as I have always lived! There has never been more than this moment for me, so what does it matter whether I have twenty-four hours or twenty-four years? It is irrelevant. I have always lived moment to moment so one moment is more than enough for me. Twenty-four hours is too much—one moment is quite enough."

The king could not understand it. The monk said, "Let me ask you, sir. Can *you* live two moments simultaneously?"

No one ever has. The only possible way to live is one moment at a time. Two moments are not given to you simultaneously; only one moment is ever in your hand. And that one moment is so flickering that if you are engrossed in the past or enchanted by the future you will not be able to catch it. It will pass you by and you will miss it. Only the mind which is receptive, here and now, can create the situation in which meditation happens.

The fourth thing is seriousness. People who think and talk about meditation take it seriously. They regard it as work, not play. But if you take meditation seriously, you cannot create the situation for it to happen. Seriousness is tension and a tense mind can never be in meditation.

You must take meditation as a game, a child's game. People who meditate should be playful—playing with existence, playing with life—weightless, non-tense; not in a doing mood but in a relaxed mood. It is only in a relaxed moment, only in a playful moment, that the happening is possible.

A serious person cannot be religious. And all religious people are so serious! It seems as if only diseased people with long faces become religious. But meditation is not something that is a "must," it is something absolutely purposeless; it is something whose end is intrinsic to it. There is nothing to be achieved by it or through it—it cannot be made a means.

But as I see it, people who become interested in meditation are not really interested in meditation, they are interested in something else and meditation is used as a means to attain it. They may be interested in silence, in achieving a non-tense state of mind—they may be interested in anything—but they are not simply interested in *meditation as such*, so they cannot be open to it.

Meditation comes only to those who are interested in meditation as an end in itself. Silence comes: that is another thing. Peace comes: that is another thing. The divine comes:

that is another thing. These are consequences, by-products; they cannot be longed for because that very longing creates tension.

The divine comes, or it would be better to say that everything becomes divine, everything becomes blissful. It comes indirectly, unlonged for, as a shadow of meditation. And this is one of the mysteries of life: that everything which is beautiful, everything which is true, everything which is lovely always comes indirectly. You cannot go after meditation, you cannot reach for it directly, because if it is approached in that way—as a longing for happiness, for the divine, or for anything else—you will lose it; it will not come and overwhelm you. It must not be made a means, it *cannot* be made a means. And seriousness is the barrier.

Meditation is play regained. Childhood has gone, but now you have regained its playful mood. You can play with coloured stones, with flowers; you can play with anything. You can just relax into a playful mood but not be playing at all. In this relaxed moment, the situation is created, the ecstasy is created, and there is the happening: the temple becomes a playhouse where everyone becomes a child playing with existence.

You ask me what yoga is and what a yogi is. A person who is meditative is a yogi: a person who lives meditatively, eats meditatively, bathes meditatively, sleeps meditatively. His whole existence, everything that he does, is meditative. He does not regard existence as a burden but as play. The yogi is not concerned with the past, he is not concerned with the future; he lives *only* in the present moment. Life becomes a constant flow with no goal to be reached, because there is no goal in playing.

Even when we play we create a goal; we destroy the playfulness and turn our play into work. Work cannot exist without a goal, play cannot exist *with* a goal. But we have become so serious that even when we play we create a goal: there is something to win, somewhere to be reached; we cannot do something just for the sake of doing it—as art for art's sake.

The moment art is for art's sake, it becomes meditative. When singing is for singing's sake, it becomes meditative. When love is for love's sake, it becomes meditative.

If the ends and the means are one, then the thing becomes meditative. But if the means are the beginning, the end is the goal and there is a continuity in between, a process in between, then it becomes work which has to be taken seriously. Then tensions, conflicts and burdens are created and your innocence is destroyed.

The means *are* the end. The end *is* the means. Anything taken with this attitude becomes meditative. The beginning is the end. Your first step is your last. Your birth is your death. Meeting is parting. These pairs are two poles of a single whole, they are one. If you see them as one, then your mind becomes meditative. Then there is no burden: life becomes just a *leela*, a play.

The cross of Jesus is a serious affair, but Krishna lived in playfulness. Krishna's dance is qualitatively different from the carrying of the cross by Jesus. The cross must have been a burden: it *had* to be carried. It was not play, it was a serious affair. That is why Christians say that Jesus never laughed. How could he laugh if he had to carry the cross? And he did not just carry it for himself, he had to carry the cross for the whole of mankind—for those who had gone and for those who were yet to come. But I don't think that this is the real picture of Jesus. This is the Christian picture, but I cannot conceive of a Christ who never laughed. If one is incapable of laughing then one is incapable of being religious.

There are, of course, different types of laughter. When one laughs at others it is irreligious, but when one begins to laugh at oneself it becomes religious. And a person who can laugh at himself cannot be serious: he is playful and then life also becomes play with no end, with no purpose; nothing has to be achieved because everything that is possible is in the present.

The achieving mind can never sever itself from the future, the achieving mind is bound to be future-oriented. And a mind that is future-oriented must be past-based, because the future is nothing but a projection of the past. We project our past memories into future longings. Our dreams of the future are our experiences of the past painted more beautifully, longed for more aesthetically.

A meditative person lives in the present, because there is no other way to live. But if you want to postpone living, you can live in the past or in the future.

Yoga is not a method of meditation but a way of creating a situation in which meditation happens. And a person who has begun to live—who lives in the moment and is not concerned with any life goals—is a yogi, a renunciate, a *sannyasin*.

Ordinarily, we think that a *sannyasin*, a renunciate, is a person who has left life. This is absolute nonsense! A *sannyasin* is the only person who has begun to live. *Sannyas* is not renunciation but initiation into living. It is a renunciation of the dead past and of the unborn future. It is a renunciation of suicidal tendencies and of the postponement of living. It is initiation into life. And yoga is nothing more than initiation into the mysteries of life and a method for creating situations in which meditation can happen.

India is not the only land that has developed yoga: whenever and wherever a person has truly *lived* he has created a yoga. Buddha had his own yoga, Mahavir and Jesus had their own yogas. So there may be thousands and thousands of different yogas.

Every person, every individual, has his own way, his own door through which he approaches reality. So no one can follow anyone else. The moment you follow, you cannot become a yogi. The follower can never be a yogi, because following again means that you are longing for security: you want to be *certain* of achieving so you follow the path of someone who has already achieved. But what was a path for someone else may not be the path for you. In fact it cannot be, because individuals are unique that everyone has to create his own path.

It is not that a path is ready-made and one just has to walk on it to reach somewhere, it is your own life which creates a path for you to walk on. You create the path and you move on it, and the more you create it, the more you move. A path created by one person cannot be trodden by anyone else because the path of yoga is inner. There are no outer markings and milestones, there are no outward signs at all. Buddha followed a certain path, but the path was an inner one which existed for him alone. No one else can move on it.

No person can ever take another person's place. You cannot die in my place. You can die *for* me—that is another thing—but you cannot replace me in my death. Even if you die for me it will be your death, chosen by you; it will not be my death.

In the same way, you cannot love in my place. There can be no substitute, there can be no help, there can be no alternative. My love is bound to be my love and my death is bound to be my death. So how can my life be your life? My life is my life; no one else can make it his way to live. It is absolutely mine, and so individual that it cannot be shared.

So everyone has his own yoga. Everyone has to create it himself. Everyone has to search in total loneliness, in total darkness. But that very search becomes the light in the dark because the very awareness of being alone destroys the loneliness and creates its own courage.

When you know *absolutely* that you are alone then there is no fear. When you know that there is no possibility of anyone else being with you then there is no fear. The fear comes with the longing, with the dream, with the imagining of the possibility that someone else can be with you. But if you are absolutely aware of the fact that you are alone, there is no fear. If this is the case, then you see that there is no way out of it.

The moment you accept your total loneliness you become a yogi and transcend society. This is the only meaning of leaving society: it does not mean that you actually leave society—no one can leave society—wherever you go, you will create it. Even with the trees, even with the animals, a family will be created and there will be a society. Society is something that follows you like an individual space: wherever you go, you create a space to live, and that space becomes a society; all those who are on the boundary of that space will become members of your society.

But in a single moment of knowing the realization that you are alone, alone to tread the path, alone to create the path, alone to be committed to living, alone to be involved in the moment, can penetrate you and society vanishes. You are alone.

There is no guru now, there is no one to be followed. There is no leader, there is no guide. You are alone; you are the loneliness. There is no one to adulterate it or contaminate it. It is so pure, innocent and beautiful. This aloneness is the path, this aloneness is meditation, this aloneness is yoga.

Still, you may ask what is to be done with this aloneness. Nothing is to be done, because every doing is nothing but an escape from it, every doing is an occupation to forget the loneliness. This aloneness is not to be escaped from and left behind. You must be deeply in it, you must remain in it, you must live with it. You must walk the path of life totally alone. Amidst the crowd, although there will be fellow travellers, you must be totally alone.

When two persons are walking on the road, they are not walking as "two," they are walking as one and one—they are two lonelinesses walking. There may be five members of a family living together: these are five lonelinesses living in a home. So live in the family but know also that you are alone.

And the moment you understand your loneliness, you become compassionate toward others and their loneliness. This compassion is the indication that a person has truly been initiated into yoga, because now that you know your loneliness, you can understand the loneliness of all.

Everyone is lonely: the husband, the wife, and the child. But they are without compassion, without sympathy; they live without loving attitudes because they are using others as an escape. The wife uses the husband as a means of escape from her loneliness, and because of this there is possession. The wife is afraid that if her husband forgets her, if he leaves her, then she will become lonely—he has become an escape for her. She is not aware of her loneliness, she does not *want* to be aware of it, so she becomes aware of her husband instead. She becomes possessive, she clings. And the husband clings in his own way, too: his wife is an escape from *his* loneliness.

We are alone. The moment this realization is there—that man is alone—then there is no escape, because then you know that no escape is possible. It is just a wish. There is no escape! The wife is just as lonely with her husband as she was without him. But we create illusory escapes, illusions of togetherness. Our families, our nations, our clubs, groups, and organizations—this whole society is an escape from our loneliness.

How ugly it is that no one thinks himself worth living with! If you are alone in your room you are bored with yourself. One bored person goes to another bored person, and together they try to transcend boredom. Mathematically, the possibility is just the opposite: the boredom is doubled. Now each bored person will be doubly bored and will think that it is the other who is at fault somehow. Each will object to the other and there will be conflicts.

A yogi, a person who has come to yoga, has come to know this naked fact: that it is everyone's nature to be absolutely alone and there is *nothing* to be done about it; one has to live alone with it. Once this awareness is accepted, there is an explosion. Now there is no need to escape because now there is no escape. He has begun to live with himself and now he can live alone but will not be lonely. He will not go to the mountains, he will not go to a cave, because now he knows that wherever he is, even in the marketplace, even in a crowd, he is alone. Now everyone looks different to him—everyone is alone! Then compassion follows, compassion for everyone's absolute loneliness.

When there is compassion for others, the yogi experiences meditation. This realization is a double-headed arrow: one end pointing to meditation, the other pointing to compassion. In your innermost world there is meditation and in your outer relationships there is compassion.

Buddha has used two words: *prajna* and *karuna*, because basically religion is concerned only with these two words. *Prajna* means meditation, the peak of knowing, and *karuna* means compassion. *Prajna*, meditation, is the flame, and *karuna*, compassion, is the light that spreads out and fills the whole world. Both come simultaneously—they are one.

Don't think in terms of this yoga or that yoga, this religion or that religion; that whole thinking is basically wrong. Think in terms of existence, life. Begin to live each moment that comes to you: live it totally, live it in total aloneness. Live life moment to moment. Be open: open to the unknown. Accept things as they come. Denial and non-acceptance are the only atheism. Acceptance—a yes-saying spirit that says *yes* to everything, that welcomes everything unconditionally—is religiousness.

Create the situation and the happening will come by itself. But it cannot be predicted. Nothing valuable can be predicted; only mechanical things can be predicted. We can predict a machine but we cannot predict life; life is unpredictable. One must simply create the situation and wait, letting things happen in their own time, in their own way.

For example, I may have prepared my home to receive a guest, but the preparation is not the guest. He may come, he may not come. The Indian word for guest, *atithi*, is very beautiful: it means a person whose coming is dateless, unknown. He may come this very moment or one may have to spend one's whole life waiting for him. This waiting is the only test: if you can wait and you are not bored with waiting—that is the only indication of your love. Now one must wait with a throbbing heart. And the waiting must continue every moment because any moment can be the moment of explosion.

One has to be aware, one has to be constantly awaiting, knowing full well that there is every possibility there may not be any happening at all, that the guest may not come.

Now, people who are incapable of waiting have created all

types of certainties. They say, "Do this and the happening is guaranteed." It cannot be! If you are certain that the guest is bound to come then you are not waiting—the certainty has killed the waiting. If the guest *has* to come, then there is no question of waiting.

With full knowledge of this possibility, in this uncertainty, the heart becomes an awaiting. Its very throbbing is an awaiting; now the very breathing is an awaiting. Every moment one is aware of everything that is happening—of the rain, the flowers, the stars. One is aware of everything, because no one knows how the guest may come. No one knows when he will come and knock at the door.

So a yogi is a person who waits and who is not asleep. Even in his sleep he is waiting, because who knows?—the guest may come while you are asleep and then he will have to go away. So a yogi is awake every moment—waiting and waiting, hoping against all hopes, certain in the face of all uncertainties. And even if for a single moment one can be totally absorbed in one's waiting! But that is not a guarantee. I can only say that it happens, and it *has* happened.

Waiting is the only arduous part because we are in so much of a hurry. This hurriedness of modern man is the only irreligiousness: it has pushed the whole of modern society in the direction of materialism. We are in such a hurry that we cannot wait, and that is the only test. We are moving so fast that we cannot stop and look for God. We are constantly running, and waiting cannot exist in a running mind.

A person who waits must be sitting, he cannot be running. If you are occupied in doing, you can escape from the waiting mind.

In Japan the word for *dhyana*, meditation, is *zazen*. *Zazen* means just sitting and waiting—doing nothing. It does not mean that you have to sit in one position for five hours; you can be occupied and still be just sitting. If you are sleeping, just sleep and wait, and do nothing else. If you are eating, eat. But then *just* eat—don't do anything else—and wait. Then everything can go on and still there is sitting, and still there is waiting, and still there is no doing. This is meditation. This is yoga.

This is not renunciation but initiation into living. I am against all kinds of so-called renunciation because they are life-denying, life-negating, anti-God. People who seem to be so engrossed with God do not really accept him totally because they deny the life that he has created. They say, "We accept you, Lord, but we deny your life." They say, "We choose between you and your world." There is no choice: life is divine, life itself is God.

One must not choose; be choiceless. Live life, be in life deeply, be involved in it, and still be alone. *You are alone.* Everything will come and go, yet your loneliness will not be destroyed because it is part of your nature. This loneliness is the basic fact from which meditation begins to grow, through which the initiation into yoga happens and, ultimately, through which a person becomes a yogi and authentically individual.

Authenticity can come only through individuality, so don't believe in dead formulas—*karma* yoga, *bhakti* yoga, *jnana* yoga, *raja* yoga. There are as many yogas, as many paths as there are persons to travel on them. Everyone must create his own yoga, only then can one's authentic being be realized; otherwise, only a borrowed, phony realization is possible.

And there are so many phony realizations. All followers reach a phony god, not the real one; they *cannot* reach the real one, because they have lost their own authentic being somewhere along the way. They are imitators and an imitator can never reach a true realization; an imitator will only realize an imitation god, a phony god. This kind of realization is simple and easy, but it won't help. Nothing will be gained by it.

There is only one true God, but there are many phony gods: the Christian God, the Hindu God, the Jaina God, the Mohammedan God, and the paths by which these religions reach God are all phony. The authentic path is *always* individual. One must be courageous enough to be oneself, to accept oneself and to jump into the unknown, discarding all that has become known, discarding all knowledge.

God is absolute aloneness. The moment you say, "Oneness with God," you create the other again. Your "God" is a means to escape from yourself—he becomes the other. The other was previously your wife, your friends. Now you have to become one with God, who is the other.

But you cannot become one with him because you already *are* one with him. Your total aloneness is the realization that *you* are God, that you are not separate from him. There can be no oneness with him, there can be no communion, because communion is possible only when there are two. When you realize your total aloneness, then it is not that now you will commune with God; now you *are* God, you are the divine! Even the language of oneness is a holdover from the dualism of the other.

Is it the mind that creates this duality?

Once you realize your total aloneness, there is no mind— the mind is your past, the mind is the other. Ordinarily, when you are alone your mind continues talking, it becomes the other; there is dialogue between your mind and yourself. But when you are totally alone, you are *alone*. Now there is no mind and there is no God; you are the divine.

So I cannot say you become one with God because to say so presupposes duality: it presupposes that God is one and you are the other. Even to say that existence is divine is to divide it; there can be no non-divine existence. It is divine-ness or it is existence; there is no need to use two terms. To say it is existence is enough; to say it is divine-ness is enough. The moment we say "divine existence" we create a division; then existence is divine and something else is not divine. But that is not the case: there is nothing that is not part of existence, nothing that is not divine.

Existence is one, so even to talk of oneness is incorrect.

That is why in India we have chosen the word *advaita:* it means "not two." It does not mean that there is one, it simply denies twoness: it says that now there are not two. Even to use the word "one" is to create the series of two, because one cannot exist without two, three and so on. Now the series will go on. But once you realize your total aloneness, in that moment you come to know that there are not two, that there have never been two.

I cannot say that you become one with God, because you have always been him; you have never been separate. Separation is your illusion; and because of that illusion you create another illusion of oneness. Separation itself is an illusion, a mental concept, and now in order to deny it you create another concept—oneness. But if the separateness is false, the oneness is also bound to be false.

You are one, not oneness. *There is no one else;* the other has gone, the other has dropped away. And when the other has dropped away, in that very moment the mind ceases. *Mind is the other,* and when there is no mind there is no other.

It is as if you were to put a barrier of earth in the middle of a river. The river is one, it has always been one, but now there is a barrier of earth dividing it. This barrier of earth is the only other: the river is one, the river-ness is one—it has always been one, it is *still* one—and when the barrier is removed the river is again one.

And this barrier creates ignorance. Because the barrier is there, we create philosophies to deny its existence. That is the difference between religion and philosophy: philosophy creates anti-barrier concepts and religion destroys the barrier.

Philosophy says that there are not two, that the twoness is false and the oneness is real. Against twoness, the concept of oneness is created. But the religious man asks: Where is the one? Where is the other? There has never been an other. The other is a concept and oneness is also a concept; both are concepts.

The reality is a concept-less, non-conceptualized existence.

So do not say "divine," do not say "God," and do not say now you have become one with him. Now there is only loneliness, there is only oneness. Now you *are;* there is no one from whom to be separate and there is no one with whom to be one. This total loneliness is *samadhi.*

Is sleep a state of loneliness?

No. Sleep as it exists is not loneliness. It is not oneness, it is not twoness, it is just unconsciousness. You are unconscious of that which is. In ordinary wakefulness you are conscious of the two. In ordinary sleep you are not conscious of oneness nor are you conscious of twoness. But in real wakefulness—in meditation, in *samadhi*—you are conscious of aloneness.

There is a similarity and there is a difference also. In sleep, you are unaware of the two but not aware of the one; in *samadhi,* in meditation, you *are* aware of it. If you can become totally aware and there is no twoness—as in sleep there is not—then oneness happens.

In sleep the mind goes to sleep. In *samadhi* the mind dies. So sleep and *samadhi* appear to be similar but they are not, because after *samadhi* there is no survival of the mind. When you awaken from your sleep in the morning your mind is strengthened, more fresh, and again duality is seen. But after *samadhi* there is no coming back. This is the point of no return: you cannot come back. Now the oneness will be eternal.

So *samadhi* and *sushupti,* dreamless sleep, have a similarity. You can say that *samadhi* is awakened *sushupti,* or you can say that *sushupti* is a sleeping *samadhi.*

TWO

Dynamic Meditation

What is Dynamic Meditation?

The first thing to be understood about Dynamic Meditation is that it is a method of creating a situation through tension in which meditation can happen. If your total being is completely tense, the only possibility that remains is relaxation. Ordinarily, one cannot go directly into relaxation, but if your whole being is at a peak of total tension then the second step comes automatically, spontaneously: silence is created.

The first three stages of the technique are done in order to achieve this climax of tension throughout all the layers of your being. The first layer is the physical body. Beyond that is the *prana sharir*, the vital body: this is your second body, the etheric body. Beyond it is the third body, the astral body.

Your vital body takes in breath as its food. If the normal intake of oxygen is changed, the vital body is bound to change. Deep, fast breathing for ten minutes in the first stage of the technique is a means of changing the whole chemistry of your vital body.

The breathing must be both deep and fast—as deep as possible and as fast as possible. If you cannot do both, then it must be fast. Fast breathing becomes a sort of hammering on the vital body and something which is asleep begins to wake: the reservoir of your energies breaks open. The breathing is like a flood of electricity throughout the whole nervous system.

So you must do the first step as vigorously, as intensely as possible. You must be in it totally; not a single fragment of you should be outside of it. Your whole being should be in the breathing in the first step.

You are just an anarchy: breathing in, breathing out. Your total mind is in the process—breath going out, breath coming in. If you are totally in it, thoughts will cease because none of your energy is available to move into thought—there is no energy left to keep them alive.

Then, when the body electricity begins to work in you, the second step begins. When bioenergy begins revolving in you, working through your nervous system, many things are possible for your body. You must be free to let the body do anything it wants to do.

This second step will be not only a state of let-go but a state of positive cooperation, too. You must cooperate with your body, because the language of the body is a symbolic one which has, ordinarily, been lost. If your body wants to dance, you cannot feel the message. So if there is a slight tendency toward dancing in the second stage, cooperate with it; only then will you understand the language.

Whatsoever happens in this second ten-minute stage, do to your maximum. Throughout the whole process of the technique, nothing should be done below the maximum. You may begin to dance, jump, laugh, or cry. Anything that happens to you, however the energy wants to express itself, cooperate with it. It will just be a hunch in the beginning, just a mild temptation—so mild that if you want to suppress it, it will not come to the conscious level at all. It can be suppressed unknowingly. So if there is any hunch, any flickering, any indication in the mind, then cooperate with it and do it to your maximum, to the very extreme.

There is tension only at the extreme, not otherwise. If the dance is not at its maximum then it will not be effective, it will lead nowhere; people dance so many times, but it leads nowhere. So the dance must be at its maximum—and un-planned, just done instinctively or intuitively; your reason or your intellect must not come in between.

In the second step just become the body, totally one with it, identified with it—just as in the first step you just become the breath. The moment you bring your activity to the maxi-mum a new, fresh feeling will surge up in you. Something will be broken: you will see your body as something apart from you; you will become just a witness to it. You do not have to try to be a witness, you just have to be identified with the body totally and allow the body to do whatever it wants to do and go wherever it wants to go.

The moment the activity is at its maximum—dancing, cry-ing, laughing, being irrational, doing any nonsense—then there is a happening: you become a witness. Now you are just watching; there is no identification, just a witnessing con-sciousness which comes on its own. You don't have to think about it, it just happens.

This is the second step of the technique. Only when the first step has been done totally, completely, can you move into the second step. It is just like the gears in a car: the first gear can be changed into the second only when the speed in first gear is at its maximum, not otherwise. It is only possible to change from second gear into the third when the speed in second gear is at its maximum. What we are involved with in Dynamic Meditation are the gears of the mind. If the physi-cal body, the first gear, is brought to its maximum extreme through breathing, then you can change into second gear. Then the second must be completely intense: involved, com-mitted, with nothing remaining behind.

When you practice Dynamic Meditation for the first time this will be difficult, because we have suppressed the body so much that a suppressed pattern of life has become natural to us. It is not natural! Look at a child: he plays with his body in quite a different way. If he is crying, he is crying intensely.

The cry of a child is a beautiful thing to hear, but the cry of an adult is ugly. Even in anger a child is beautiful; he has a total intensity. But when an adult is angry he is ugly; he is not total. And any type of intensity is beautiful.

This second step is only difficult because we have suppressed so much in the body, but if you cooperate with the body then the forgotten language is remembered again. You become a child. And when you become a child again a new feeling comes to you: you become weightless—an unsuppressed body becomes weightless.

When the body becomes totally unsuppressed, suppressions that have been accumulated throughout your life are thrown out. This is catharsis. A person who goes through this catharsis can never become insane; it is impossible. And if an insane person can be persuaded to do it he will return to normality. A person who has gone through this process has gone beyond madness: the potential seed has been killed, has been burnt out through all this catharsis.

This second step is psychotherapeutic. One can only go into meditation by going through catharsis. One must be cleansed completely; *everything* nonsensical must be thrown out. Our civilization has taught us to suppress, to keep things inside, so that everything goes into the unconscious and becomes part and parcel of the soul and creates much havoc throughout the whole being.

Every ghost that has been suppressed becomes a potential seed for insanity. This must be eliminated. As man becomes more civilized, he becomes potentially more mad. One who is uncivilized is potentially less mad because he still understands the language of the body, he still cooperates with it. His body is not suppressed; his body is the flowering of his being.

This second step must be done totally. You must not be outside the body; you must be in it. When you are doing something, do it completely: be the doing, not the doer. That is what is meant by totality: be the doing, become the act; don't be an actor. An actor is always outside his acting, he is never in it. When I love you I am in it, but when I act lovingly I am outside the act.

In the second step so many things are possible—something different will happen to each individual. One person will begin to dance, another person will begin to cry. One will become naked, another will begin to jump and yet another will begin to laugh. Anything is possible.

Move from within, move totally, and then you can proceed to the third stage.

The third stage is reached as a result of an inherent sequence. In the first stage, the body electricity, or you can call it *kundalini*, is awakened. It begins to revolve and move. Only then can the body be in a total let-go, not before. Only when the inner movement has begun are outer movements possible.

When the catharsis of the second stage is brought to a peak, to a climax, the third ten-minute stage begins. Begin to repeat vigorously the Sufi mantra: *hoo! hoo! hoo!* The energy that has been awakened through breathing and expressed through catharsis now begins to move inward and upward; the mantra rechannels the energy. Before it was moving downward and outward; now it begins to move inward and upward.

Go on hammering the sound within—*hoo! hoo! hoo!*—until the whole being becomes nothing but the sound. You must exhaust yourself completely; only then does the fourth stage, the meditation, happen.

The fourth stage is *nothing*—only silence and waiting. If you have moved into the first three stages totally, completely, holding nothing back, then in the fourth stage you will automatically fall into a deep relaxation. The body is exhausted; all suppressions have been thrown out, all thoughts have been thrown out. Now relaxation comes spontaneously—you need not do anything to make it happen. This is the beginning of meditation.

The situation has been created: *you* are not there. Now meditation can happen. You are open, waiting, receptive. And the happening happens.

The people who come to me for spiritual guidance are people of a disciplined mind. How can people such as this practice Dynamic Meditation with its explosive expression of emotions?

Such people cling to discipline, but the primary need of an unstill mind is to be anarchic; only then can it transcend itself. You can ordain discipline, but discipline is an outward conditioning—the inner being remains the same. There will be anarchy within and discipline without: anarchy remains in the heart while the discipline forms a part of the cultivated personality. So first let tension, confusion, anarchy, reach a climax. Then there will be an explosion, and discipline will come as the result.

Tell the people who come to you for spiritual guidance about this method. They will feel the change that happens through it themselves, the transformation. Let them practice it as an experiment—with their unstill minds, with their doubts—and if something happens through it, then the practice will continue by itself; there will be no need to convince them.

The anarchy within must be exploded. It should not be stilled or pushed down, it must be expressed in total intensity. Calmness, serenity, *nirvana,* come not by stilling the mind but by explosion. Then the stillness comes by itself; it is not a cultivated composure.

You must express what you are totally. Of course, that will mean madness, because you are mad. If you allow yourself to express what is inside you, the madness will come out. You will feel strange about it: what will be expressed is something which is unknown even to you. But *it is your expression*—the authentic expression of what is within you.

So many things that must be expressed have been suppressed in the unconscious. They have been suppressed for centuries, through many past births. The anarchic being that is within each of us is unknown even to ourselves. It must come out, the ghost inside us must come out. And it can come out only when it is expressed—expressed in total intensity from the innermost core of being. First one has to become mad in order to transcend one's inner madness.

Let Dynamic Meditation be tried as an experiment by those who come to you. Tell them that the emphasis is not on believing it, but that they should do it, then they will know what happens. And things are bound to happen, because this madness that I am talking about is within everyone.

Is there some kind of hypnosis involved in the technique?

The moment a person begins to experiment with this method there is no question of belief or faith, there is no question of hypnosis. The contrary is the case: we have hypnotized ourselves into believing that we are normal and sane human beings. *This* is the hypnosis! The whole world is a great madhouse and we have hypnotized ourselves into thinking that we are sane, normal. But the insanity that is hidden in the background always tries to come out: it erupts, it explodes out of us in dreams.

It explodes out of us when we are intoxicated. LSD or mescaline cause an explosion of madness, but the explosion does not come from the LSD or mescaline, and dreams do not create the madness either. Drugs or dreams just uncover your self, the authentic being that is within you. That is why, for a *sadhaka*, a seeker, it has been an essential part of many old traditions to know the self through drugs: various intoxicants are known to have been used in order to know the inner being, to know that which is within.

It is total nonsense even to try to discipline the mind. You have not known the innermost core, you are cultivating disci-

pline from the outside—you will become disciplined but the
madness will always remain within you. The ultimate outcome will be schizophrenia: there will be two beings living
simultaneously within you, your whole being will be split.
There will be continuous indecision and conflict within. And
remember, conflict dissipates energy. So the first step toward a
harmony and unity of the being is not discipline but knowledge of that which is within.

The within has been so suppressed for centuries, for millennia, that this suppression has become a part of your self.
And not only you but the whole of humanity has suppressed
what is within; you are just a part of the process. You have
not suppressed what is within you consciously, knowingly—it
is part of your heritage to do that.

That is the reason for the fear about this technique. The
inhibited, suppressed, collective mind is the basis of all insanity, all tensions, all conflicts, all disharmony. There is a
lurking fear that if we allow ourselves to let go, something
which has been hitherto suppressed will emerge. And it is
bound to happen. This fear creates a doubt about the technique, and the doubt then becomes another instrument for
suppression.

So tell your students not to believe in the technique but
just try it as an experiment for fifteen days. Let them try it for
an hour a day—beginning with ten minutes of deep, fast
breathing—and things will begin to move.

The breath should be both deeper and faster than *bhas-
trika* breathing. No rhythm is to be used with the breathing.
If you try to use any rhythmic method, the explosion will not
take place because you will still be disciplining yourself. So let
the breathing be as anarchic as it can be: the only emphasis is
on rapidity, intensity, and depth. Don't remain outside the
breathing. The total being must be involved in it—a total
commitment with no holding back.

When you are totally involved in it your whole body and
mind begin to vibrate, the body electricity begins to move.

When you feel something in your body that you have never felt before then the technique has reached you. Then no doubt remains, because you have experienced something which you have never known before.

We never feel our body electricity. That too is a suppressed part of our personality: not only the mind is suppressed but the body also. We are not in our bodies as much as nature has prescribed; we have suppressed our body wisdom.

Once someone begins to vibrate because of the deep, fast breathing done in the first stage of the technique, his body electricity begins to move. In that moment he moves out of the grip of society: his bioenergy is so powerful that you cannot force him to conform. When the energy grows to its own awakening you never feel that you are just existing, that you are a slave to your condition. You feel yourself to be something unbounded, something unlimited, something powerful. In this moment, people have declared themselves to be God: *aham Brahmasmi*, "I am Brahman."

The first feeling of *aham Brahmasmi*, "I am God," comes from feeling the movement of electricity that is ordinarily lying dormant in the body stimulated by the deep, fast, intense, breathing. Then every experience that comes through the body becomes authentic.

We call something real because we feel it through the body. I say that you are real because I can see you, I can touch you. If I cannot touch you then you are a hallucination; I cannot believe in you. If I cannot touch you I cannot show you to others. Our reality is that which can be validated through the body.

Any technique that opens up a new dimension of experience for the body becomes real to us. Then there is no more doubt about the technique and one can proceed further.

That is why I emphasize the breathing in the first step. Then, in the second step, the breathing will continue on its own. Meanwhile there will be many reactions in the body;

they may take many forms, but they will all be *happenings;* they will not come through discipline. And so many things *will* happen!

How should one sit when practicing the technique?

You can sit in any position but it is better if you are standing. The eyes should be closed and the technique should be done on an empty stomach.

In the second step, relax the body. Give it freedom; don't suppress it. Go on breathing and allow the body to move, to vibrate, to dance, weep, laugh. Let whatever happens, happen: the body will take its own course and many things will begin to happen. Then, in the third step, while still breathing intensely and allowing your body to do whatsoever it wants to do, begin to repeat the Sufi mantra—*hoo! hoo! hoo!*—with no gaps between the sound.

This must be done as vigorously as possible—so that you know you are not withholding any energy. Involve yourself totally. By and by, the repetition of the sound will become more and more vigorous, more and more intense.

During the first step, the total attention must be on the breathing. And when you breathe deeply the second step will emerge as an outcome of the first: the body begins to move. You are not to relax even for a moment; continuous effort is to be there. Then relax into the second stage, allowing your body the freedom to express whatever has been held back in the past. The body will begin to move, to dance, etcetera, and soon you will begin to feel that you are something separate from the body. You will see the body weeping, laughing, crying so clearly that you will not be able to identify yourself with the one who is doing all this. You will see yourself jumping, dancing: something is happening mechanically. You will begin to see the body as a separate entity. It is only when the

body becomes an automaton that the consciousness feels itself to be separate; until then there is always identification
with the body.

Why are we normally not able to feel dis-identified with the body?

You are totally identified with your body because normally there is no gap between you and your body. What you
are doing, your body is doing, and vice versa. You and the
doings of your body are identified as one and the same. But
when the body takes its own course, it becomes an automaton. Things begin to happen which you had never planned,
which you never thought possible. "Am I doing this? Am I
feeling this?" And you know that you are not doing it. You
did not will it but still the dance goes on—and vigorously, too.

Then there is a gap. The gap between the doer and the
doing is there: you are not doing it. Now the body has become an automaton.

Consciousness cannot identify itself with an automaton.
You cannot identify yourself with a machine unless the machine works according to your will. If I tell this microphone to
move and it begins to move, there is every possibility that I
may identify myself with it. Now it has become part and
parcel of me: it moves when I ask it to move. The hand moves
when I tell it to move, and when I tell it not to move it does
not. That is the basis of identification: through the movement, the mover and the moved have become one.

But when the body moves without your conscious exer-
tion then it becomes a separate machine. Only then can you
see that you are separate from the body. This is such a distinct feeling that no confusion remains.

That is why I emphasize body movement. Let it happen.
Whatever happens, let go. You will see that your body has
become like that of a madman, or an animal, or a machine,

and you will not be able to identify with it, so you remain aloof. Now you begin to be a witness.

In the second step of the technique you begin to witness all that is happening. The body is moving, the hands are moving, forming many *mudras—mudras* that you have never known or planned. Your inner witness comes into being. You begin to see the happenings as something outside yourself; now you are not the doer but just a seer. There is no question of your doing anything; you begin to *see*.

In the beginning the identification with the body may be there, but as you allow yourself to let go more and more into the technique, action vanishes. If the body falls to the ground you will not think that you have fallen but that the body has fallen.

Then, in the third step you are to shout *hoo! hoo! hoo!* with total intensity. You must become completely mad. Move deeper and deeper into the sound. Bring your effort to a peak, because only from the peak can you fall to the very depths of your being. The more mad you become, the higher the peak of intensity that you reach, the deeper will be the depths that you fall into and the more sanity there will be.

Real sanity is that which comes after the transcendence of madness. Relaxation comes only when you have come to a peak of tension. Then the fourth stage is reached: the mind becomes calm, quiet.

Now, after having gone through the three previous stages, of ten minutes each, you are just to relax for ten minutes. Stop everything that you have been doing in the first three stages and just fall down or stop in place, remaining frozen in whatever position you are in. Now there is nothing to do. There is no question of doing anything because you will be completely exhausted, your whole being will be tired. Now let-go becomes an automatic process.

The technique is a sequence of stages, each following automatically from the preceding stage. If you continue the technique and do not add the fourth stage it will come by itself as a natural consequence of what has gone before. It is bound to—a moment is bound to come when everything is exhausted and you fall down. There is nothing left to do.

The fourth stage is the moment of non-doing. That is what I call *dhyana*, meditation. The first three stages are only steps; the fourth stage is the door. Then you *are*. There is nothing to do—neither breathing nor movement nor sound. Just silence.

The three previous stages must be "done" in a sense, but the fourth stage comes of its own accord. Then something happens that is not your doing. It comes as a grace: you have become a vacuum, an emptiness, and something fills you. Something spiritual pours into you when you are not.

You are not there because there is no doing; the ego disappears when there is no doer. The doer is the ego. So *you* can be in the first three steps because you are doing something—breathing, moving, shouting—but now, in the fourth stage, *you* cannot be, because there is no doing.

The ego is nothing but an accumulation of your memories of past actions, so the more a person has done, the more egocentric he is. Even if your doing has been in social service or religious work, whatsoever you have done becomes part of the ego. Ego is not an entity but the memory of your doings, so in those moments when there is no doing, you are not. Then, something happens. Even though you are not doing anything you are totally conscious. Silent, but conscious. Exhausted, but conscious. Only consciousness is there: a consciousness of your deep let-go, a consciousness that now everything has disappeared.

When the fourth stage has ended, when it becomes a memory, then you can recollect it. But in the moment itself there is nothing, there is only consciousness. Because only nothingness is there, you cannot be conscious of anything. Afterward you recognize that there has been a gap. Your mind functioned until a particular moment; then there was a gap, and then it began again. You feel this gap afterward: the gap, the interval, becomes a part of your memory.

Our memory records events and this gap is a great event, it

is a great phenomenon. Mind is a mechanism. It records everything; it is just like the tape recorder that we are using here. The recorder will record two things: when we speak, the words are recorded; and when we are not speaking, the silence, the gap, is also recorded. Even when we are not speaking, something is being recorded—the silence, the gap. In the same way, the mechanism of the mind is always there recording everything. In fact, it is even more keen, more sensitive, when there is a gap. The tape recorder can blur what I am saying, but it cannot blur my silence. The gap will be recorded more intensely; there is no possibility of error.

So the gap is remembered—and the gap is blissful. In a way, a memorable event is a burden, a tension, while the gap is a calm, blissful interval. This gap is *dhyana*, meditation.

Does one experience various things in this fourth stage?

Experience, as such, is psychic. There is no such thing really as "spiritual experience." It is only a gap. The experiencer is not there, so you cannot use the terminology of experience. You experience a moment which is of no-experience. As far as language can indicate it, I can only say that it is a gap.

Every type of indication is bound to be negative. Language is for events, it is not for silence. If I try to express what happens in meditation through the medium of language, the terms I will use will depend on me—and one term will be as meaningless as any other because the experience cannot be indicated by words. So you may call it *Brahman*, you may call it *nirvana*, or anything you like, but it will just be a choice between different names.

Every name is as meaningless as any other, so every type of religious language—Christian, Hindu, or Buddhist—will be equally meaningless. The only similarity, the essential unity in all religions, is that their languages are equally erroneous. They are bound to be so. This is not a condemnation, it is a fact—because the gap cannot be expressed, it can only be felt. And feeling has no language; it has no words.

If ego evaporates in the fourth stage, then what happens after the fourth stage is over and one comes back from meditation?

The ego returns, because the whole mechanism is still there. It has not died; the whole past is still there. For a while you were not part of it, for a few minutes you transcended the mind, the ego. You were beyond it. You left the house; now you have come back. But you cannot come back as the same person who left it because you now have known something beyond. You cannot be the same again, but still you come back.

The easier it becomes to go out and come in, the more likely it is that a new stage will begin in which you are neither out nor in: you transcend both. This is the culmination, because then you can be out when you want to go out and you can be in when you want to come in. You are neither in nor out; you transcend both. This is *samadhi*.

When I can come or go as I choose, when I can be in or out, when it becomes easier and easier for the mind to be here or not to be here according to my preference, then both the inner and the outer can be transcended. Only then is the innermost core reached. That is *samadhi*. What happens in the fourth stage is only a glimpse of it. In Zen Buddhism, this glimpse is called *satori*. *Satori* is not *samadhi*, *satori* is just a glimpse, because you can still come back from it. But you cannot come back from *samadhi*: it is the point of no return.

What happens to someone who reaches samadhi?

If you say "somebody reaches," then somebody is there. Only when somebody is *not* there, is absent, does he reach.

Somebody moves into meditation, somebody comes out of meditation—that is the feeling of the soul. But *nobody reaches samadhi*, because when *samadhi* is reached, nobody is there.

There are many religions which have stopped at the point reached in the fourth stage of Dynamic Meditation, so they say that there is a soul, the *atman*, because all they have known is the coming in and the going out of the soul. But the fourth stage is just a glimpse. You go out—you leave the body, the mind, the ego—and you come back again. It is not the point of no return; there is every possibility of coming back.

You come back because the whole mechanism is still there waiting for you. You come back and again the whole thing begins to work. All that is left then is the memory of the gap. But that gap calls you back again and again.

Some religions such as Zen have mistaken this *satori*, this glimpse, for the ultimate experience, for *samadhi*. It is not *samadhi* because there is still a possibility of coming back. The ego did not die, you only jumped away from it temporarily. For a moment you were out of its grip, but now you are back again. *Satori* is just a jump. Don't become attached to it.

You can become attached to the outward jump very easily because it is so blissful there. Each time you move into the experience it gives you a certain freshness, it thrills you. But then you go on repeating the experience of going into meditation, feeling its bliss, and coming back. By and by it becomes a routine, and when you come back you think that you have achieved the ultimate experience possible because the experience was so blissful. But you have not yet known something *beyond bliss*, so each experience of meditation becomes part of the same repetitive, mechanical, routine groove. Now even the gap, even meditation, becomes part of your mechanical functioning.

There are religions that have stopped at this point, hence they say that there is a soul, an *individual* soul; they cannot conceive of *Brahman*. *Brahman* only comes after you have gone beyond the fourth stage—when you can go out and come back in and do not become attached to the bliss of the gap. And once you begin to witness this going out and coming in, the meditative state of mind and non-meditative state of mind, you have reached the most delicate point. Then you know that this too is a habit which you can prolong for many lives. It is not *samadhi*, it is not ultimate awareness; it is *satori*.

When you start observing this, a silent awareness begins to descend in you. Silent awareness, choiceless awareness, is possible only at this point, never before.

Do you mean after satori?

Yes. Only after *satori*, never before that. When you become silently aware of the going out and the coming in of the ego, the ultimate explosion can happen. You go beyond "out" and "in"; you dissolve in the explosion.

This is the point of *nirvana, brahma-upalabdhi, moksha,* or whatever you want to call it. It has never been recorded by the mind; it can never be recorded because the mechanism itself has dissolved.

After this does one continue to live in the body?

Certainly, because the working of the body is another process. It has a process of its own; one can live in it or one can go out of it. To others it seems as though one is still living in the house, but for the resident the house is no longer there. The whole universe becomes the body.

Is there still an individual body?

No. It only seems so to others. If I try to talk about it, to verbalize it, then the whole thing becomes a problem. Whenever we talk about what happens when one goes beyond meditation, it becomes a paradox. It can never be explained because any type of explanation will create new paradoxes, new contradictions.

This "fifth stage" is an explosion of everything that has been. Now *nothing* remains. It is an explosion of the totality that you were: your memory, your intellect, your ego, your personality, your being, your soul. Everything that you were is now not; you just go beyond. There is no *you*; you become everything. That is the point of *Braman*, cosmic consciousness.

Dynamic Meditation can lead you only up to the fourth stage, *satori*. The fifth is beyond method. Guidance is possible only up to the fourth stage. That is why Krishnamurti talks of no-guidance. The fifth stage is beyond guidance. Silent awareness is always beyond guidance. Either it happens, or it doesn't happen.

This fifth stage is existence itself.

Every day Buddha was asked the same question: "What happens to an enlightened person? Where does he go? Does he exist or not?"

When Buddha was asked this same thing persistently, he said, "It is irrelevant. Do not ask. This is a question that must not be asked." He listed eleven questions which he could not be asked, and this question was one of them. It is not that Buddha did not know; he would not answer because any type of statement was bound to create new problems.

What is the purpose of life? Why should we practice yoga or any meditation technique or discipline? What should one's mission in life be?

Life is a mystery which cannot be solved. If it could be solved, it would not be a mystery. There is no mission in life, because there can be no mission in a mystery; there can simply be playfulness, a *leela*.

This whole existence is just a play of energy. "Play" means something that is purposeless or something that is its own purpose. There is nothing to be achieved; the very act is the achievement. Life has no mission, because living itself is the achievement. So you can live in many ways, you can do many things.

It is all just an outflow of energy, a purposeless cosmic play. That is why it is a mystery.

The West is more intent on discovering new things than the East. It is more curious, more inquiring, but it could never develop a religious consciousness because it could never conceive of life as being purposeless. We have been able to see sense in nonsense, we have been able to see no-purpose as having its own purpose, its own intrinsic value. Life is, that's all. Existence is; it is enough. Why ask for more? How can there be anything more than existence?

When you reach *satori* this feeling of the purposelessness of life begins to dawn upon you: life becomes a play. That is why Zen monks are gay and not serious. A serious person is one who has never felt the miraculous, the mysterious, so a serious person can never be religious. At the stage where *satori* has begun to happen, you become playful. Life becomes just a joke; there is no seriousness about it. You can laugh at it. A Zen monk can even laugh at the Buddha. And it is beautiful, so beautiful—nothing like it has ever been achieved anywhere else.

People are afraid to come to this state because they know it will disturb the pattern of society.

It disturbs because society is created by people suffering from the disease called seriousness. The whole of society is dominated by this particular disease. It has dominated everything: everything has been put into a pattern, categorized; everything has been demarcated.

Play cannot be demarcated. When I love somebody it is

play. But when it becomes a marriage then the play has gone; it has become a serious affair. Love is always playful, that's why it is always momentary; it comes and goes. But marriage is something static; it comes and never goes. It is a plan, a demarcation, a fixed pattern.

Are you saying that marriage cannot be spiritual?

It cannot be. Marriage can never be spiritual because it is a fixed thing. But I have used marriage just as an example. In fact, the whole of society can never be spiritual because it is based on rules. Rules are always serious; you cannot be playful about them.

When Bodhidharma reached China, he put one shoe on his head and the other on his foot. The Emperor asked, "What are you doing? What nonsense!"
Bodhidharma said, "I am joking."
The Emperor said, "But we never expected a joking, laughing *sadhu*."
Bodhidharma said, "How is it possible for a *sadhu* to be serious? God is not serious, he is so unceasingly playful!"

Creativity comes out of playfulness, hence so much creativity is born out of *satori*.

Does satori bring inner knowledge?

The desire for inner knowledge, the desire for this experience or that experience, is part and parcel of the seriousness-disease. The serious mind even tries to categorize religious experience; it wants to become the authority: "I have inner knowledge. I know, and you don't know. I will teach you." Again, the mind is attempting to recreate the pattern of the serious society. Do you see it? Religious societies have been created only for this purpose. Sects, ashrams, monasteries, etcetera, are alternative societies.

But the spiritual person is always playful. His life is just play, he is not serious about anything that he does.

And nothing new ever comes out of seriousness. Seriousness can only repeat the old because it always thinks in terms of security, in terms of rules; and rules come from the old, from tradition—they cannot be invented daily. A playful mind is spontaneous. It has no rules, so it is always insecure; it is always on the verge of losing everything, because *there is no security.*

Once a person has begun to experience *satori,* every type of seriousness becomes nonsense. That is the only indication there is that meditation has happened, and that is why a person who achieves *satori* becomes rebellious. There is no other reason. He becomes rebellious because he has to rebel against all types of seriousness.

But if people become rebellious, how can society control them?

It is the very concept of control that has made the whole world a mess. The moment you think in terms of control, you begin to suppress and you begin to destroy individuals and create types. And, paradoxically, when you destroy individuals and create patterns and types, much disorder follows. But this disorder is not because of rebellious minds, it is just a reaction against the dead order.

If the rebellious mind wins even for a single day, there will be no disorder because there will be no order; order and disorder are two sides of the same coin. A person who tries to create order creates disorder: the attitude, the mind that tries to ordain discipline creates indiscipline, too.

Your ego reacts against a person who is trying to discipline you, but this is reaction not rebellion. Rebellion only emerges after *satori,* so there are not many rebellious persons—only a Jesus, a Buddha, a Socrates, very few. But there are many reactionaries. For example, the communists—people like Marx, Bakunin, Lenin, or Mao—are all reactionaries, they are not rebellious. A rebellious person is a phenomenon: only when you are rebellious are you really alive. And if the whole world were to become rebellious . . .

Every type of invention, every discovery, always comes out of playfulness. Einstein, Archimedes, Newton, and others were all playing. Many things happen when you are not serious, when you are not concentrating, when your mind is in a let-go.

Newton was sitting under an apple tree. An apple fell, and something happened. Archimedes was lying in his bathtub, and something happened. He jumped out of the tub crying, *"Eureka! Eureka!* I've found it, I've found it!" Einstein was very fond of playing with soap bubbles. His concept of the expanding universe came to him through playing with soap bubbles, watching them expanding and dissolving.

The history of humanity is not the history of the masses, the conformists, the serious, the lawgivers, the ruled and the rulers. The masses have not created a single masterpiece— neither invention nor painting nor poetry nor music. But a few evolved ones who were not serious about their lives have been creative. Discovery has always come through unknown people who were just playing with their lives. If they had been serious they would have preferred to do business, to start a factory or something.

So the first thing is to play with your life. Then so many phenomenal things happen. Religion, science, art—everything comes out of a non-serious, playful mind.

There is no purpose in life, no mission in life. Life is enough! It is more than enough. Every sense of mission must go because it is anti-life: all propaganda is nothing but politics in the garb of religion, a mission, an ideal. Leadership, gurus, disciples—all this is nonsense. If you practice Dynamic Meditation, if you allow yourself to pass through a catharsis and move into a total let-go, your concept of a mission in life is bound to go.

So practice Dynamic Meditation. Do it to your fullest capacity—take it to a peak. You must go mad completely; only then will authentic sanity come, and only then will others begin to be helped by you.

THREE

Yoga: A Spontaneous Happening

Is the practicing of traditional asanas helpful for meditation?

Man's personality is neither solely physical nor solely mental but both simultaneously. Rather, it would be correct to say that it is psychosomatic. There is no gap between the two, so anything that happens on the physical plane vibrates on the mental plane and vice versa. Philosophers have been in the habit of thinking of man as only body or only mind, or both parallel but separate, but not as one. To me, and to present-day science, they are one.

The visible mind is the body and the invisible body is the mind. These are two polarities of one existence. "Mind" means something that transcends our senses and is outside the grip of our senses. "Body" means something that comes within the grip of our senses. The division between the two is due to the senses and their limitations.

Man's existence is both body and mind simultaneously. Even to say "both simultaneously" is inadequate. The two are the same. The difference is only of vibrations. "Body" is the gross vibration that can be received through the senses and "mind" is the subtle vibration that transcends the capacity of the senses.

Why am I saying this? There is a well-known theory in

Western psychology known as the James-Lange theory. Common sense has always understood that body follows mind: when you are in fear, the body begins to run away; when you are in anger, your body begins to prepare for fight. But the psychologists, James and Lange, proposed quite a contrary view: that it is not fear that creates running, but running that creates fear.

According to them it is the body comes first; mind follows. Their argument is that you cannot be fearful or angry if no corresponding body situation is created. So they have argued that you can only prove that anger is something mental if you can be angry without your body's responding to it. They claim that it is impossible to find anger in you if your eyes are not red and your fists are not ready to fight.

But James and Lange are not right even though their theory seems very plausible. There *are* body reactions—and without body reactions no mental attitudes can be expressed—but that does not mean that mental attitudes cannot *exist* without body reactions.

One can show symptoms of anger as far as the body is concerned and yet be without anger . . . like an actor. An actor can be completely acting anger—and as far as his body is concerned anger is there—but there is no anger within him. In the same way he can show all the symptoms of love by his appearance and yet not feel love. The body can express without the mind's feeling it.

The mind can also feel without the body's expressing it, because the gross is within our control whereas the subtle is not. Whenever we observe anger we observe it through the body—not only somebody else's anger but our own as well. The anger still exists in seed form, it is there as a potential, but we cannot even detect it ourselves until it is manifested on the gross plane of the body.

This theory of James-Lange is fifty-percent correct—common sense is always fifty-percent correct—but what James and Lange came to know and propagate has been known to yoga for centuries. That is why *asanas* and *mudras* were developed. Yoga had already come to understand that everything mental has a corresponding situation in the body, and when the mind changes, the body assumes the corresponding postures, *mudras*, expressions, and is transformed.

Yoga also taught that the contrary is possible: if the body takes a particular posture, the corresponding mental attitude will be produced in the mind. But that is as wrong as the James-Lange theory—you may be just acting: a person can sit in the same posture as Buddha, but that does not mean that Buddha's inner tranquillity has been produced. On the other hand, if someone has Buddha's attitude, his body will assume a posture that is similar to Buddha's on its own.

That is why I am against practicing all *asanas*. They must come by themselves or you must not do them. If you do them, there is no guarantee that the corresponding inner state of mind will follow, and it will become a gesture, an act—that's easy for us. You can sit like Buddha or stand like Mahavir—there is no problem in it—but it is meaningless; nothing is accomplished by it.

Where did these *asanas* come from? Whenever the state of mind that Buddha had is there, the body follows it with a particular posture. It must follow it, it will have to follow it. This has been known for centuries—that there are particular outward gestures that correspond to particular mental states—so it was surmised that if we create these postures and gestures in the body, the corresponding mental states will definitely follow.

That is not necessarily so. On the contrary, it is a very dangerous assumption because you can go on acting and not only will others be deceived, you will also be deceived. That is the real danger.

If you sit in Buddha's posture, the position of the body will create a feeling of tranquillity in you. Now you will assume that tranquillity has been achieved: you will feel still, silent. But this stillness, this silence, is just a deception; it has not come to you, you have imposed it on yourself; it is not from within but from without. It will feel very good, but it is a created, conditioned stillness that has been produced and projected by the body.

We have been doing this for so many lives—it is the same thing we do in our ordinary, day-to-day life. You just smile without feeling it; it is simply a gesture. But once you smile, a feeling comes. This feeling is very false, but you yourself are deceived by it. Without feeling any love, you can show love and others will be deceived. But there is every possibility that you will forget it is just a gesture and will be deceived into thinking that you have been loving. Then an authentic love— which is a revolution, which is a death, a total transformation—will never be possible because of your gesture, your imitation.

So I am totally against *asanas* or *mudras;* they must not be practiced. If they come, it is all right. They *will* come, but let them come by themselves; then they will be important indications. Then they will not be deceptions but rather landmarks, symbols which indicate something to you and to others.

But let them come from within, do not impose them from without. If you impose them on yourself, they may not be exactly what is needed or required by your particular individual situation, because they are generalized forms. If you reach Buddhahood, a particular *asana,* a particular gesture, will follow. But it will never be the same *asana* as Gautama Buddha's, something will be essentially different. It will be like it in a general way, but you are not Gautama Buddha—your whole individuality, the whole mechanism of your mind and body is different—so it will never be exactly the same. If you impose Buddha's posture on yourself, it will not correspond to *your* individual situation. There are so many *asanas*—they will not occur to everyone.

Mahavir attained *samadhi* sitting in a very different position, *goduhasan:* it looks just like a milkmaid when she is milking a cow. No one else has ever reached *samadhi* in that position—no one sits like that! But it is possible to sit like that for aeons and aeons. And as far as *samadhi* is concerned, nothing is in any way irrational or illogical.

Why was Mahavir sitting in that position? Buddha's posture is all right, but Mahavir's posture is very absurd. He was not practicing it; it came. Something happened within him and his body took on a certain posture—although a very absurd posture. If he had been practicing *asanas* he would have been sitting just like Buddha, because that was the traditional meditation posture. But he was in an attitude of let-go, and *samadhi* came and created a posture that was particularly required for his body and his individuality.

Everyone will need to express himself individually. No person is like any other and no one can be. An individual is unique so that everything that flowers in him will flower in an individual and unique way. If you impose something from without, then it will be a generalized conception; it can never be fitting and harmonious to your situation.

So when I say I am against *asanas*, I am not saying that there is no reason for them, I am not saying that they are absurd; what I am saying is that *practicing* them is absurd. Let them come—they will come—and when they come by themselves they will have a reason of their own. They will work within your body and through them your body will become attuned to a new situation.

You cannot go to sleep standing on your head. You cannot, because sleep needs a particular body posture. If you lie down it does not necessarily mean that sleep must come, but when sleep comes, you will be lying down. What I am saying is just like that. You must not begin from without; the beginning must be from within. The flowering is going to be without, but the roots must begin from the inner core of your existence. You must begin with meditation and let everything else follow. Whenever a particular *asana* is required, it will come. And when it is no longer needed, it will go by itself.

Sometimes in the second stage of Dynamic Meditation I start doing asanas. I can't tell whether I'm doing them because I want to practice them or whether they are coming of their own accord. How is one to know the difference?

Don't think about the difference; just let them come. When they come by themselves in meditation, let them come, and then they will go by themselves. But if they are coming because you are practicing them, then they will never go.

When the need is over, when the need is fulfilled, they will wither away by themselves. So don't think about it. You cannot know beforehand whether they are coming out of habit or not. If they are authentic, then when the need is fulfilled they will go. You will not know this while you are doing the *asanas*—you will not be able to tell the difference— but by and by the difference will be felt.

When you practice a particular *asana* it is very different from when it comes to you spontaneously. The distinction is subtle but it is always there. When you are doing it, it will be a disciplined act following a particular routine, a form, an order. When it comes by itself there will be no discipline in it, there will be no order in it, it will be a chaotic act. And only when it is chaotic is it helpful.

A disciplined act is not helpful because it is always a function of the conscious mind; it never goes deep. Only when an act is chaotic does it become deep, and only then can it reach the unconscious, because the unconscious mind is a chaos, a great chaos.

The unconscious is just like the beginning of the world. Everything exists in a potential form in the unconscious, but it has not as yet taken form and shape; everything is hazy, cloudy, uncertain. If you try to impose some set pattern on it, you will not achieve anything. You will only go on circling around your conscious mind, because the conscious can be forced into discipline while the unconscious can never be forced into discipline. But the unconscious is the root, the unconscious is the source.

Meditation means going into the unconscious: diving into it, being in it. It is to be chaotic in the chaos. It is to be without form within the formless. It is to let go of oneself, to float in the clouds, untethered; to let oneself move into an unmapped territory, an uncharted sea. Don't go into it with a disciplined mind or you will never go.

You move in circles in your conscious mind: you go on repeating and it becomes a habit; you have just aligned yourself with your conscious mind. A disciplined mind is always a poor mind because it will never greet chaos. It has never been outside the limits of the conscious, it never transcends the conscious; it is not concerned with the infinite.

A man with a disciplined mind may be a great man, like Gandhi, but he will have a small mind because his total concern is with the conscious mind and with discipline. He will never move into the undisciplined—he will never touch it.

The conscious mind is just like a garden growing beside your house, it is never like a forest. And the unconscious is like a dense forest that has no boundary. You can never know the boundaries of the unconscious, so there is every possibility of being lost. To remain in the conscious mind is safe; there is no risk. To move into the unconscious is risky. Courage is needed.

So do not discipline your body and do not discipline your mind. Live with the undisciplined, live with the chaotic, live with danger. That is what meditation means to me: to live in insecurity, to live in chaos, to live in the limitless.

But that does not mean that a discipline will not come to you. It will come, but it will come *as freedom*. It will be an alive discipline from within: always touching the unlimited, always potentially chaotic, always explosive, always in the unknown—a moment-to-moment discipline. It will seem very inconsistent without but it will have its own consistency, there will be an inner consistency running through it.

If you discipline yourself from without, there is every possibility that you will never come to know the unconscious. And the conscious mind is no mind at all, it is not life at all.

It is just a utilitarian instrument developed because of society; it is not you. But because we have to live with others, we need certain things that can be known about us and can be relied upon: discipline, a particular character. The conscious mind exists because of the relationship between you and others. It is just a link between you and all those with whom you are related, but it does not help you in relating to yourself, in knowing yourself.

I remember a story. King Ashoka sent his son to Ceylon to take them the message of Buddha. He met the king of Ceylon and asked him a question: "There are people in the world to whom you are related and others to whom you are not related. These are the two categories. Is anyone left who is not in one of these two categories?"

The king said, "I am left."

Ashoka's son said, "Now the message can be delivered to you. You are an intelligent person, so something can be said to you. I asked this question to find out if you know that there is something else besides the related and the unrelated or whether you think everything belongs to one of these two categories."

This third—which is neither related to you nor unrelated to you—is the unconscious part of your existence; it is the realm of meditation. The conscious mind is a help as far as your relationship or non-relationship to the world is concerned, but it can never be a help as far as *you* are concerned.

Meditation does not mean a conscious implementation; it means an effortless jump into yourself. With discipline, you can go step by step, but you can never discipline a jump. The first three steps of Dynamic Meditation are not steps of meditation at all, but steps that lead you to the place where you can jump.

Real meditation is a jump—a jump into the unknown. So do not discipline your body; let it go where it wants to go. Allow yourself to move into the unknown. Things will happen, *asanas* will be there, but only those which are required by you. Now *asanas* may come to you—*asanas* which are not normally depicted, which have not been described so far—because the possibilities are infinite and the *asana* descriptions we have are only of the more commonly experienced postures. There are also infinite *mudras*. They too will follow.

Let the *asanas* come and go; don't practice them and don't cling to them. Let them come by themselves, let them go by themselves; don't be concerned with them at all. That is what I mean when I say I am against all *asanas*: that you should not be concerned with them at all.

One thing more: *asanas* have a cathartic value. Ordinarily, our mind works only in relation to someone or some situation. That means our mind only reacts to things, it never acts. And if a person begins to act without a stimulus we put him in a madhouse, because his actions seem absurd, nonsensical. If he begins to *act*, that means he is not acting in relation to any situation, he is acting from within.

So much is suppressed in us because we cannot act, we always have to wait for situations to react to. If you are angry, you cannot just be angry, you have to wait for the proper situation to arise—someone must create a situation which you can react to. If you begin to be angry without provocation, you will be called mad. Even when you are reacting you look mad, and if you are reacting to something that has happened, then you are justified to yourself and others. But if your action is not a reaction, then there seems to be no justification for it; you simply look mad.

So much inside you needs expression and is never expressed because no situation arises for it to be expressed. You go on suppressing what is inside you, fighting against it. You cannot express love to the empty air, so when the opportunity to love is not there, love is suppressed. Then a curious phenomenon begins to happen. You are full of love but you cannot express it to the air. Then someone comes along to whom you *can* be loving but with whom you are not in love and you begin to act. The real is suppressed and the unreal is acted upon. In this way, your whole life becomes a confusion.

Catharsis is needed in meditation because of two things. One: your suppressed vibrations, attitudes, moods, actions, and *mudras* must be released—not as reactions but as autonomous actions; not related to anybody else but as overflowing energy. In Dynamic Meditation they can be released, unaddressed.

You begin to cry, you begin to laugh. Only when it is unaddressed can the expression be total. Then you do not need any justification for it: it is its own justification. Whatever you are expressing you can express totally; there is no need to suppress it. Now you are talking to the sky, loving the air; you are angry with the gods. Unrelated, unaddressed. Then you become totally expressive and the suppressed mind is lost. This is catharsis. You need to be able to express without situations, because the human mind is so suppressed that if you only express when there are situations for it you will never be rid of suppression.

Two: if catharsis is allowed you will stop acting, because acting is a substitute, part and parcel of suppression. Your circumstances and your needs do not coincide. When the need is there, the circumstance is unfavorable, and when the circumstances are favorable, your need has long since passed. You are forced to be inauthentic, forced to act.

When catharsis takes place in meditation, you will begin to feel a new life surging within you. You will never be able to act again. Now you will be bold enough to laugh without reason and bold enough to be angry without there being any person, any situation, present. Then a second boldness will follow: you will be bold enough *not* to act. That is one of the greatest signs of courage: not to act. Then your personality begins to be authentic. And this authenticity can only come to you after catharsis.

Real *asanas* and *mudras* are a catharsis, an expression, an overflowing. And the more they overflow, the more weightless you begin to be. Then a day comes when you are completely weightless; a moment comes when you are not bound by gravity. Weightless! Only in this weightlessness does the flight of the alone to the alone take place.

If you practice *asanas* there will be no catharsis, only suppression. That is the basic difference: if you practice *asanas* they will be suppressive, but if they come to you spontaneously they will be expressive, there will be a catharsis.

If you impose *asanas* on yourself, the action is just part and parcel of your total suppressive routine. If you impose *asanas* which your mind is not ready for, you will force your body into a particular posture and the body will have to follow your will. This type of exercise, if done to its logical conclusion, will create a split in the personality. Then you will become two: the one who is suppressed and the one who is suppressing.

Yoga, to me, means becoming one, not two. It is integration, not splitting. I call an *asana* "*yogasana*" only when it comes automatically. If it is imposed, then it is not concerned with yoga at all. Yogic exercises are gymnastics, not yoga. That is why I have not used the word "yoga" but have been using the word "*asana.*"

Yogasana is an *asana* which has come to you, which has happened to you; otherwise an *asana* is no different from anything else that is imposed on you, any physical discipline. It may prove health-giving but it can never prove spiritual; it can never help to integrate you. The health benefits that you derive will be at a very high cost because your personality will be splitting in two. The whole nature of the experience of those people who practice *asanas* begins to be less and less spiritual and more and more physical.

And this is a curious phenomenon: these *asanas* seem to be meditation-oriented—they are supposed to be—yet all over the world, wherever *asanas* are talked about, *dhyana*, meditation, is the least talked about subject. Now the whole thing has become topsy-turvy: they teach meditation along with *asanas* as if meditation were only another *asana*. It is not an *asana* at all. Meditation is the ground, it is the base, it is the seed. Everything must be meditation-oriented, because meditation is first and everything else follows.

After doing Dynamic Meditation will I be able to meditate more deeply as time goes on?

As time goes on, you will begin to have more depth. You will be able to go deeper and deeper, just like a person who is digging a well. He goes on digging with the same implements, with the same speed, with the same method. By and by all the earth is removed and the well goes deep, deep, deep—until a moment comes when the waters rush forth.

The eternal waters are there—you have only to remove the layers of earth completely. Go on digging in the same way, with the same method, with the same implements. Don't bother about any changes, the layers of earth are the same; just remove them completely. The water is there deep within, waiting for you, the water of the deep unconscious. Between you and your unconscious mind is a layer of earth, a great layer of suppressed vibrations, suppressed thoughts created by you as a barrier against the insecurities and aggression of the unconscious. You yourself have created this barrier, so you have to go on digging.

As time passes you may not feel that you are progressing, because you can feel it only when the water has been reached, only when the inner sources explode. Otherwise you will still be digging the dry earth. And yet it is not the same earth, for what you have dug up and thrown away is no longer there. But there is still more earth that has to be dug up.

This digging only concerns you and your meditation; it is not concerned with the explosion itself. Explosion comes as the climax, it comes in a single moment. It explodes in you, you explode with it. It is a happening beyond time.

So just go on digging. The job will be boring and monotonous. When there is something to be achieved at each step the work is never boring—you are getting results, so your ambition urges you on so that more and more can be achieved. But up to a certain point in meditation everything is a bore, everything is monotonous. It seems to be the same, although it is not the same. You are going deeper and deeper every moment, but you can never judge what depths you have gone to until the depths explode within you.

When that happens, within that moment you will know that the process is complete. Until then you are just groping in the dark, hoping against hope, while nothing seems to be coming out of it. Then it comes all at once. Depth is not achieved step by step as far as meditation itself is concerned. Either it is there, or it is not.

So you will have to be patient with it. And, naturally, with every individual seeker the time it takes will be different. No one knows how much earth you have accumulated between you and your depths. It may be that the layer is very thin and only one attempt will break it open. It may be that the layer is dense and you have spent lives and lives building it up. So it will depend with each individual.

But one thing is important: patience—patience and work without hoping for results. Work without hoping for results *means* patience. If you long for results, if you hanker after them, then the goal is lost. It is really impatience which asks for a result. But if you go on practicing the meditation technique patiently, that in itself will bring about the change. Perseverance without any expectation is a great transformation in itself. Even if meditation is not achieved you will change, because to be patient and to do something without asking for results requires great stamina, a great power of endurance. This stamina will gradually gain in strength.

Because of the whole layer of suppression that exists between you and your innermost depths, time will be needed before the explosion can happen. If you are not totally patient and strong in your determination, you will not be able to bear the shock of explosion. The explosion of bliss is so intense that it requires a deep capacity to contain it; it requires a strong inner will.

A very powerful will is required, so even if the layer between you and your depths is thin it will take time in order for your will to strengthen. A person who can bear to live without results becomes capable of achieving great results; otherwise he is not qualified for the great moment. If bliss comes to you when you are unprepared for it, it will be unbearable. You will go mad and lose your balance forever. It is a great phenomenon, it is a cosmic phenomenon. It is the sea pouring into a drop! You must be prepared for it, and this preparation comes when you labor patiently, ceaselessly.

Ask for no results; wait patiently. That is what is really meant by *shraddha*. It is not faith in any particular thing, it is faith in oneself. It is not belief in somebody else but belief in oneself.

As time goes by, you will go deep. This is not because time has passed but because of your patience—because you have persevered in spite of the monotony, expecting no results. With nothing gained, you still kept on going, you still kept on with unflagging zeal. This creates will, and this makes you capable of bearing the explosion when it comes. To be impregnated with the cosmic, a particular maturity is needed— just as a certain maturity is needed for pregnancy. In this spiritual impregnation the cosmic comes to you: it is the rebirth of yourself.

In India they say that the *brahmin*, the *kshatriya* and the *vaishya* are twice-born and the *shudra* is once-born. I say: *he who is once-born is a shudra*; a person who has not achieved a second birth, a rebirth, is a *shudra*. So we are all *shudras*, untouchables, because the divine has not touched us. But this rebirth will come if you are patient and sincere. Wait for it, pray for it, hope for it, but do not be in a hurry.

Is it necessary to pass through psychic stages before the explosion can happen?

No, it is not necessary to pass through psychic realms. But that does not mean that you will not pass through them. You can pass through them with such speed that you do not notice them or you can pass through them slowly, taking each and every possible step in the psychic world. You have to pass through the psychic realms because they lie between you and your innermost depths—between you as you are and you as you will be. But you can pass through them with such jet speed that you never experience them or you can pass through them at a bullock cart's pace. If you want to see the landscape it is better to ride in a bullock cart.

There are bullock cart methods and there are jet methods. The method I am talking about, Dynamic Meditation, is a jet method: you will pass through these realms and not know it because you will be going at such great speed.

But if you are longing for psychic powers, even unconsciously, then even with a jet method you will behave as if you are in a bullock cart. If you have a keen desire to develop psychic powers then as you pass them you will be caught by them.

We have inner longings that we are not even aware of. Our mind is basically power-seeking: whether it seeks power in the outer world or the inner, it is always seeking power. One must be careful not to seek power. The psychic realm is there, and if you are seeking powers then you will be caught in them somewhere.

The outer world cannot give you as much power as the inner world—there is a great potential of power within. In fact there is so much atomic energy within a single human body that if it were to explode and release its total energy the whole world and its population could be destroyed.

Physicists talk about atomic energy, yogis talk about psychic energy, but the energy is the same—only the approach is different. Physicists approach through the atoms of the body; yoga approaches through the atoms of the psyche. Both these approaches are two poles of the same thing.

Yoga approaches from the inner, so the yogi talks about psychic powers. They are there, but if you seek them you will be caught in them, which will be pathetic, pitiable, because when you reach the psychic you are very near to the cosmic, to absolute bliss. You are near to the flower, but you have shut your hands on it. So one must beware.

In Dynamic Meditation you do not have to become alert to the psychic because it is a jet method: it goes so fast that you will pass the psychic realm without noticing it. But still, because all that we have read and heard is stored and accumulated in our minds, we must be cautious of psychic powers. They are there, but they are not of much significance in themselves.

The power-seeking mind can never be at ease because the power-seeking mind is basically violent. Violence needs power: we want to be above others, we want power, prestige, heights. This can happen through atomic energy or psychic energy, by becoming a political leader or a spiritual guide. But a violent mind can never be spiritual—at its lowest the power will be physical, at its highest it can be psychic. But if one is seeking truth, bliss, if one is seeking the divine, then this power must not be sought. You must deny this power, you must be meek. As Jesus said, "Blessed are the meek, for they shall inherit the earth."

But you must not be meek *so that* you will inherit the earth. If that is the reason, if that is your desire, then you will not be meek. A meek person means a humble person; he is not seeking power, he has left that dimension completely. He is poor in this sense: he is no one. Only one who is no one can become one who is everyone. Only one who is no one can become that one who is all.

Power must not be sought, must not be longed for. When it comes your way, just be a witness to it and pass on. Don't linger for a single moment because even that pause, that standing near it, will prove fatal. It corrupts. Power corrupts not because it is bad in itself but because we are after it. The saying is: ". . . and absolute power corrupts absolutely." Outer power cannot corrupt as much as inner power can. It is much more absolute in a sense, much more independent of others, so it can prove to be a great stronghold for the ego.

Outer power is always dependent on others. You are never absolute, you are never sovereign; you are always dependent. Someone somewhere far away can be the cause of your fall. Hitler achieved that power which is based entirely on outer forces. Such people build a great pyramid and stand on the peak, but they are completely dependent on the pyramid so they are always fearful. A single brick thrown out of the pyramid, and down they come.

Inner power becomes absolute in the sense that you are not dependent on anybody else. You are the sole master of it so it becomes more egocentric. Outer power has corrupted man, but inner power has corrupted him more. It is not power itself that corrupts, because the divine also is power; rather, it is the seeking, longing ego which corrupts. If we are corrupt, then when power comes our corruption will be exposed. Before that it remains hidden. To be corrupt we need power.

So one must beware of inner psychic forces. They exist, but do not look at them. Just pass them by, just be a witness to them. They will be with you, they will work in you, but they will be like shadows—they will follow you. Things will begin to happen around you but you will not be conscious of them; you will not be strengthening your ego through them.

With this method you will pass through psychic planes, but with much speed. All that is between you and your innermost depths will be there, but just as a shadow following you. There will be *siddhis*, there will be happenings, things will begin to change, but your power will be felt by others, not by you. If someone says that something has happened to him because of you, you will look up and say, "Because of him, not because of me. I am no one." When Jesus learned from people that they were healed because of his touch, he said, "Not because of me but because of Him. I am no one. I am just a servant, I am just his instrument."

Then there will be powers, but they will not be ego-centered: they will be God-oriented and God-centered. But you must not be concerned with them. When they come, just pass by and bid them farewell.

FOUR

LSD: A Shortcut to False SAMADHI

In experimenting with LSD I have experienced states which seem to be similar to descriptions I have read of samadhi. I could feel my kundalini rising and my chakras opening up. I felt a oneness with the whole cosmos. Were these genuine experiences of samadhi? Is permanent self-realization possible through the use of LSD? Is there any harm in using LSD as an aid to meditation?

Your experiences were not genuine. They were not in *samadhi*, they were just chemical changes. The mind can project anything it wants to project—even an unconscious desire for *samadhi*. Then, whatever you have known or read about *samadhi* will be projected through the chemical help of LSD.

LSD or any other chemical drug is nothing but a help in making the mind more projective. All the hindrances, all the ordinary hindrances, are withdrawn: reason is withdrawn, the conscious mind is withdrawn; you are completely in the grip of the unconscious. But by itself the unconscious will not bring you to *samadhi* through the use of LSD; an experience like this is only possible if the unconscious has been fed certain preconceptions: colors, particular experiences, this and that. Everything in the unconscious can be projected, but if you have not known anything about *kundalini* or *samadhi* beforehand it is impossible to feel them through LSD.

A person who is suffering from a phobia will project his phobia. A person who has suppressed his fear about something will feel that the very thing he is afraid of is taking place. So LSD will bring different experiences to different people. It can only help you to project what is already inside your unconscious mind in seed form. If it is love, then love will be projected; if it is hatred, then hatred will be projected. LSD is a mind-expanding drug—whatever is inside you in seed form will be expanded into a tree.

You could feel *kundalini*, you could feel *chakras*, you could feel a harmony or oneness with the totality, only because these seeds were already in your unconscious mind. If they had not been there then LSD would not have projected these things.

This is not a genuine experience of *samadhi*. This "*samadhi*" comes from your unconscious longing. LSD can help anything that is unconscious to be realized physically. So what you have experienced is something that you wanted to realize projected on the psychic canvas. It is not a spiritual revelation, it is not *samadhi*, it is not genuine. It is nothing but a dream; it is just a dreaming phenomenon.

You dream in the night because the barriers of the conscious mind are withdrawn. Whatever is suppressed in your mind, desired, longed for, begins to take shape and form; you begin to imagine it. But while you are dreaming you never know that it is a dream. It is so lifelike, it is so authentically real that you can never conceive that it is only a dream.

LSD is a chemical way of dreaming; it is not a natural way. Through LSD you can see things that you have not known, realize things that you have never realized. But all these realizations are only apparent realizations; they are not real. They are beautiful, they have their own charm, just like a nice dream.

But LSD can project a nightmare also. It depends on you,

not the LSD. If your mind is tortured, fragmented, and many untoward images are suppressed in it, that is what will be projected. There are persons who have seen hell on an LSD trip, there are persons who have seen demons. It depends on the person. All that a chemical drug can do is to project whatever is there to be projected.

Do not mistake your experiences on LSD for *samadhi*. And do not cling to such experiences or they will be an obstacle to meditation. You have felt so much through LSD dreams that when you enter into a real state of meditation it will seem faint in comparison. The experience of meditation is not so vital, you will not feel such a great upsurge of energy. This will then create a mood of depression because you will feel that something is being lost—that you have known something and this "something" is not coming to you through meditation. Then the mind will say, "LSD is better." And if you go on taking LSD, your mind will become less and less meditative, and meditation and its experiences will go on becoming fainter and fainter.

So don't take LSD again. It may have been just an experiment, but it has made an impact on your mind. That impact is dangerous because you will always be comparing: real meditation will seem unreal to you because the unreal has appeared to you as authentic.

Then, too, your comparison can never be accurate, because you cannot remember exactly what you have seen on your LSD trip once you are out of it. Just as you cannot remember a dream exactly, once you have awakened. Now you imagine the dream again—you add much to it. In the same way, when you are no longer under the influence of the LSD, you cannot remember it exactly as it was; there will only be a faint feeling of blissfulness. Now you will imagine the whole experience again, but this will not be exactly the experience that you had. It can never be. You have a feeling that you have seen something, that you have known something. That feeling is illusory.

A certain blissfulness can be revealed to you through the

use of a chemical drug. Because of the drug, you are totally relaxed; your tensions, at that moment, are withdrawn. It is not that they no longer exist—they are waiting to come back to you—but they are not in focus, so you relax totally. The revelation of bliss which comes when you are absolutely non-tense is so great that you will continue to experience a blissful feeling afterward as a hangover. In this bliss, you will imagine again what you have seen, what you have known, but now ninety percent of it will be imagination.

The greater the distance between the experience and the memory, the more beautiful, the more blissful it will look to you. It will become a cherished remembrance. Now each time you meditate it will be a faint thing in comparison because meditation is real, it is not a dream. Its progress is step by step, it is not so sudden. It will never overtake you. In between, you will be preparing so the progress will be very slow.

Time exists in the real world, but in LSD experiences or in ordinary dreams time does not exist as it does in our waking hours. In a single moment you can dream a dream that would take many years to happen in reality. And it happens so suddenly that it overwhelms you; it shatters your total memory. For a moment, all tensions are non-existent. You are relaxed and a cosmic harmony is felt. Barriers are not there: you don't exist as an "I"; you and the world have become one. This is so sudden and blissful that each time you compare the cherished memory of it with reality you will go on adding to it: the memory will become more and more beautiful and the reality will become fainter.

Don't compare meditation to what happens on LSD. First of all, you cannot compare it because they are two different states of mind and the faint remembrance of one state cannot be brought to another. Secondly, when you compare what has happened retrospectively, it is the same unconscious mind which has projected these experiences that is doing the comparing. You are the one who has taken LSD and you are the one who is meditating: in either case the same unconscious seeds are there.

Another thing to be remembered is: don't have any pre-formulated, ready-made concepts about meditation and don't think about what the result of it is to be. To go into meditation is to go into an uncharted sea; you cannot know beforehand what is going to happen. If you already know what is going to happen it will begin to happen, but it will just be a projection. You can project in LSD and you can project in meditation because the unconscious itself is the projector.

All your knowledge about *kundalini,* all your knowledge about *chakras,* all the knowledge that you have of *knowing* must be thrown out because, even without the help of chemicals, your ordinary mind can project these things. When you are meditating you can project the same thing that you can project with LSD. The process will be slower because there is no chemical help, but the phenomenon is the same.

I am not saying that there is no such thing as *kundalini,* or *chakras.* I am not saying that no experiences happen; there *are* experiences but you must not know about them beforehand, otherwise you will project them. You must be completely unknowing, you must be ignorant: that is the basic condition to proceed further. Each thing must be known and experienced directly; it must not be taken for granted. Information should not be confused with knowledge.

So throw away all information. Cease to "know" things and proceed as if in a vacuum, proceed in ignorance. You don't know, so everything will be a surprise. Everything *must* be a surprise. If it is not a surprise, if you say, "Yes, I have known this before, it has happened before," then you have not moved into the unknown, you have not moved into meditation.

There is a great possibility of self-delusion. The mind is deceptive and the unconscious goes on playing tricks. And the deception is possible not only on LSD but even in ordinary meditation, because the unconscious mind is the same. If you want to move into meditation, you must change the unconscious. It must become vacant; it must not be a "knowing" unconscious. It must be open, vulnerable, ready to face the unknown, because meditation means going into the unknown.

Before meditation can happen you need first to go through a purging, a cleansing: you need to be completely overhauled. The unconscious must not be burdened, it must not have seeds: *sabeej samadhi* is *samadhi* with seed. "*Samadhi* with seed" means a *samadhi* with all your projections. It is not *samadhi* at all; it is just a name.

There is another term: *nirbeej samadhi*, "*samadhi* which is seedless." Only a seedless *samadhi* is authentic because there is nothing being projected. You are not projecting; something has come to you, you have encountered something. You come to know something completely new, completely fresh, absolutely unknown before. It is not even imagined, because whatever you can imagine you can project.

Knowledge is a hindrance to *samadhi*, so a person who "knows" can never reach *samadhi*. You must not go into meditation burdened with knowledge. You can reach the door of *samadhi* only if you are completely empty-handed, naked, vacant. Only then does the authentic thing happen; otherwise, you will be meditating with all your projections.

You have been projecting in meditation and you have been projecting in your LSD experiences. Both are projections. You must unburden yourself; understand that. Forget all that you have known; don't conceive of *samadhi* in any way whatsoever. Don't have any preconceptions, don't conceptualize. Just move innocently, like a child, into an unknown country where the language is not known, where you are not acquainted with anything, where everything is new, and you have no guidebook with you. Only in this way will things begin to happen that are authentic.

Otherwise it will take a long time before something authentic happens to you in meditation. You will bypass the reality completely and the projections will continue. Then LSD will be more forceful, more vital, and meditation will be faint in comparison. But if you unburden yourself of your knowledge, if you forget these names—*kundalini, chakras,* everything—if you put it all aside and proceed just like a child, then meditation will happen. Otherwise meditation, too, will be imaginary, a dream.

The difference is very subtle. It is difficult to know what the difference is, but there *is* a difference. One thing about it can be understood: if things are happening according to your knowledge, according to what you *think* should be happening, then you must not take them seriously. They can never happen according to your knowledge, they happen to each individual so differently that no scripture, no guru, can say exactly what will happen. Everything that has been said is just a generalization; it happens to no one in exactly the same way. The experience of the seven *chakras* or the passage of *kundalini* is so different for each individual that if things are happening according to a pattern you must not take them seriously; you are imagining them. Things will be different for you; they will never be the same as with anyone else. The happening is individual and there are no generalizations.

Everybody's experiences are different, incomparable. Everything said about these things is a generalization. Generalizations never happen. For example, there are twenty people here. We can calculate the average age of everyone here, but no one may be exactly that age. The average is a myth; it is a generalization. We can determine the average height of everyone here, but no one will correspond to it exactly. We can calculate the average knowledge, but no one may possess it.

All generalizations are myths. They help to formulate things, but they don't help to lead you to the reality of life itself. They help you to make systems, they help you to make scriptures, they help you to make maps, but you should never confuse the map with the country itself. You may have seen a map of India, but nowhere in India will you find what you have seen on the map. When you enter India you will never encounter the map; it is just a generalization. It helps you to formulate an idea of India, but it never helps you to experience the country itself. Rather, it becomes obstructive. The experience is hidden behind the formulation, the preconception.

Knowledge can be gathered without your knowing that knowledge is dangerous. If the knowledge is concerned with outside information that is all right, it makes no difference, but if it is concerned with inner experiences it makes a lot of difference—because the mind projects.

Begin to meditate as if you had never heard anything about *kundalini* or *chakras*. Go into meditation without this information. Make it a first condition that when you enter meditation you are not supposed to know anything. You are just to be ready, open to anything that happens. There is nothing to expect, nothing to compare your experience to.

First, your preconceived ideas must go. You must not cling to them. If you don't cling to them they will go, they will die. The seed will burn and die. But if you cling to it, it will seem like knowledge, it will seem to be a help, a guide. Don't cling to your knowledge and it will not remain alive in you. Then it will not project itself.

Secondly, forget about your LSD experiences as if they were dreams; otherwise they will continue to come between you and your meditation and the comparison will go on. That comparison will be suicidal: if you continue to compare, meditation will cease and you will be more and more disposed toward using LSD. But a chemical help can only create a psychic phenomenon, it can never be an authentic realization. Realization is not something that has happened to you, it is *something to which you have happened*. It is not that something has penetrated you, it is something that you yourself jump into.

With LSD, you go nowhere; you remain just where you were and something happens to you because of the chemical change. Through a chemical agent your ordinary mind, your ordinary reasoning, is no longer functioning; the ordinary restrictions that you place on the unconscious become numb.

They are turned off and the unconscious is turned on. But you are not the controller, the chemical agent is the controller. You are under its influence, you are not a free agent—now the LSD is free to work inside you. It is not that you are working but that you are being worked upon: something is happening *to* you, not you that are happening to something.

Realization means that you have happened to something: you have jumped, you have encountered something. You are no longer the same person you were, you have changed. This change is a conscious change, with full awareness. And the change is because of your effort. You have done something, you have travelled, you have gone to some peak.

There are two ways to experience yourself on the peak of Mount Everest. The first is to imagine that you are on Everest but still be lying there in your bed and not really go anywhere. The second way is really to climb to the peak. The very going will create a change in you. The very struggle to climb to the peak will change you so that the peak will not only be the peak of Everest but will also be the peak of your efforts. When you have reached the top of Everest, you will have reached the Everest of your will-power.

In your dreams you have gone nowhere. You exist in the same state, in the same time as you were before. The only thing that happened is that a dream has come to you. The dream can come in two ways: it can come through meditation or you can create it through LSD. That is why the experiences in both look similar—because you can create these experiences in either way. Only if the unconscious is not burdened—only if it is not filled with longings and suppressions that are waiting to be projected—is meditation possible.

Another difference is that when you have taken LSD your conscious mind has gone to sleep and your unconscious mind takes charge of you and begins to work. But in meditation your conscious mind does not go to sleep; rather, your conscious mind expands until your unconscious also becomes conscious. The light of the conscious moves deeper and deeper into the unconscious until a time comes when there is no separation between the conscious and the unconscious; your whole mind is one. Then meditation has happened.

During my LSD experiences I saw a particular sequence of colors: saffron, then yellow, then white, then a deep blue. What do these colors mean?

There is some meaning to it, but the order is always different for different people. Still, it has a meaning. Colors, perfumes, sounds—everything has a meaning.

The first thing to be noted is this: as you go deeply inward, each of your senses has a corresponding inner manifestation. For example, your eyes. They see what is without, but when you close your eyes you are able to see that which is within. The essence of every outward experience is also stored within; all your senses have reservoirs of experience stored in your mind. When you travel inward, these reservoirs will be encountered. When you come to the reservoir of colors you will see beautiful colors such as you have never seen before with your eyes. These are the essence of all your past experience of colors.

It is just as when a painter paints a beautiful woman. It is not any particular woman—he has seen so many women. His painting portrays the essence of them all. All that he has seen, all that he has known, is being depicted in this one figure. Something in the woman is from one source and something else is from another source, but the particular figure itself is nowhere to be found. It is not imaginary and yet it is nowhere to be found: it is authentic because it has been taken from experience, and yet it is just an image. It is both real and unreal.

Our senses have stored all the experiences not only of this life but of all the lives that we have lived. These essences remain in us. The eyes have stored colors, light, etc.; the ears have stored sounds, harmonies, silences, etc. All the senses have their own storerooms within the brain.

Now even science confirms this: if you touch a particular brain cell with an electrode the brain cell will explode. A person who falls down may see stars if the particular brain cells which store light experiences are affected by the fall. Your memories can be affected by the touch of an electrode. If I touch a cell in which the memory of your childhood is stored you will again become a child and everything that you experienced as a child will be replayed on the canvas of the mind.

When you go inward, these essences explode within you and you experience many things which are unknown in the outward world in such a pure form. The outward world is always impure, but inward experience is a pure essence; it is just an electrical phenomenon. Because the phenomenon is just energy, it is pure. Nothing obstructs it: it is transparent.

But don't take these experiences seriously. They are only meaningful insofar as they are indications that you are going deep. They are only part of the scenery on the way, they are not the destination itself. When you really reach deep within there will be no experiences—neither of light nor of sound nor of anything else.

Unless all these experiences cease, you cannot transcend the mind. These experiences are just the psyche displaying the accumulation of what it has preserved throughout endless lives. That is why each person will feel different things: each one has a different accumulated past, so each one will have a different orientation as far as his senses are concerned.

Two days ago someone with no sense of taste came to see me. He has never known what taste means so he cannot experience taste deep within himself. There are people who are blind or color-blind—in fact, one person in twelve is color-blind: he sees everything else, but he cannot see one particular color.

Bernard Shaw, for example, could not make any distinction between yellow and green. He was color-blind as far as yellow was concerned, so in his inner experiences he could never see yellow. There was no reservoir of the color yellow in him; there was no essence of yellow. He had never seen it, so to him it was non-existent.

We do not see every color. The seven colors that we can see are not all the colors that exist—beyond those seven we are color-blind. Below and beyond these seven colors are infinite ranges of colors. We have not seen them so we will not experience them in our inner journey. All that is felt or experienced is what we have stored within us of the outer world.

If a musician goes into meditation he will experience sounds that a non-musician can never know. A painter will experience colors that a non-painter can never know. If someone like Van Gogh were to go into meditation, we cannot conceive of the colors he would see or what new combinations he would know.

This, too, will differ from individual to individual. Only one thing is certain: when you go deep within on your own inner path, things will begin to happen. You will have experiences of colors, sounds, smells, which are all stored experiences. The whole mind is a storehouse and every cell is a bundle of experiences ready to explode. Go inside, touch the source, and it will explode.

These experiences are meaningful inasmuch as they indicate that you are moving inward. But because the feeling that you have experienced is lovely, the mind will long to cling to it. You will want to repeat it and that will be a hindrance to further progress.

A state of mind is to be reached where there is no experience. Rather than saying "a state of mind with no experiences," you can say "a state of mind in which one experiences nothingness." Experience itself is the last barrier. One must come to a point where one is, and there is no experience.

Only when experiencing has ceased does duality cease. When you are experiencing something, duality is still there. *You* are there, so the experience is there—something without is there. Even if you experience oneness with the world, this experience is part of duality.

When meditation comes to a full flowering, there will be no experience at all. You will *be,* and *just being* is the experience. Nothing exists—only your being, only your existence. And when there is no experience, the experiencer explodes. He can exist only in opposition to some experience. When the object is not, the subject itself explodes—there is no subject, no object.

Only then is the existential achieved. Only then can you say God is. You are not and the world is not. God is! That very "is-ness" is God.

But these experiences will come. They are not meaningful, but they will come.

I have been trying to meditate for a long time, but I am not getting any clear results. What's wrong with me?

There can be many reasons. It may be that the meditation method you are using is wrong or that the way in which you are practicing it is wrong. Or it may be that neither the method nor the way you are practicing it is wrong, but the unconscious longing behind the method is wrong. Then the unconscious must be changed.

If you have been using a method for many years and only getting shallow results, change the method. There are so many methods of meditation that one should not cling to only one method. There may be nothing wrong with the method, but as far as you are concerned it may be wrong.

So change the method. Change is always helpful. If one becomes accustomed to a method, the experiences one has through it will be shallow. And when nothing new is happening but you go on repeating the method as a routine you will never achieve anything through it; nothing significant *can* be achieved.

My method of Dynamic Meditation is such that it can never become a routine. It is so disorderly and chaotic that you can never make a routine out of it. Methods of meditation with a disciplined and orderly system behind them always become routine. You must use a chaotic method so that you are never settled in it. Then it will always remain new with something new to be faced each day.

The method I have been talking to you about, Dynamic Meditation, will help you because it is chaotic. No *disciplined* method can be helpful to the modern mind, because the modern mind is basically chaotic: it is constantly changing.

The old mind was an unchanging, fixed mind. A person was always settled. Two centuries ago a person who was born a Christian would die a Christian. Today it is not so—a person born a Christian may become a Hindu: everything has become chaotic. The childhood mind of a person is one thing, his mind during youth may be something else. One day he may be a communist and at a later date he may go to the Himalayas to meditate.

Today's mind is not fixed; it is in chaos. So all the old methods which were meant for fixed minds are out of date. For the chaotic mind, a chaotic method is needed; only then can you be led into deeper realms. Otherwise, the results are bound to be shallow. Once you settle into a technique you become bored with it and if you go on prolonging your practice, it will be suicidal. Don't continue to practice a technique that is not helping you. The method is for you, not you for the method. If something is not working for you, change it.

Practice Dynamic Meditation and awareness of breathing. In a very short time you will feel the change that is happening inside you. But you need a chaotic method—one that will not become routine.

FIVE

The Vital Balance

In our civilization, professional people like me have a particular problem: we make too much use of our intelligence. So much so that we tend to view life through the intellect only, thus negating all other means of doing so. This tends to make life boring and dull, and robs it of its luster.

No one can use his intellect too much. It is such a great force, with so much potential, that you cannot use it too much. Not only do you not use it too much, but you never even use it totally. Ordinarily, you do not use more than ten to fifteen percent of your total intellectual potential.

And another thing: when you do intellectual work it does not necessarily mean that you are using your intelligence. Intellectual work, too, is mechanical. Once you acquire the know-how, no intelligence is required at all; the mind works just like a computer.

The real problem is not the use of too much intelligence but the non-use of emotion. Emotion is completely disregarded in our civilization, so the balance is lost and a lopsided personality develops. If emotion is also used, then there is no imbalance.

A balance of emotion and intellect must be maintained in

the proper ratio, otherwise the whole personality gets diseased. It is just like using only one leg. You may keep on using it, but you get nowhere; you simply tire yourself. The other leg must be used. Emotion and intellect are like two wings: when we use only one wing the outcome will be frustration. Then the bliss that comes from using both wings simultaneously, in balance and harmony, is never attained.

Don't be afraid of using the intellect too much. Only when intelligence is used do you touch the depths; only there is your potential stimulated. Intellectual work does not mean that your intelligence is being used—intellectual work is merely superficial, no depth is touched, nothing is challenged. That gives rise to boredom: it creates work that is without enjoyment. Enjoyment always comes when your individuality is challenged and you have to prove yourself and respond to the challenge. When challenged, intelligence or emotion both create their own bliss.

A person is schizophrenic if only one part of his personality is working and the other is dead. Then even the part that is working will not work really well because it will be overworked. Personality is a totality; it has no division at all. Actually, the whole personality is a flowing energy. When energy is used in a logical way it becomes intelligence, and when it is not used logically but emotionally it becomes the heart. These are two separate things; it is the same energy flowing through two different channels.

When there is no heart but only intellect, you can never relax. Relaxation means that now the same energy within you is working in a different channel. Relaxation never means no-work; it means work in another dimension. Then the dimension that is overtaxed relaxes.

A person who follows an intellectual pursuit continuously never relaxes. He does not divert his energy to another dimension so his mind goes on working in only one direction unnecessarily. That creates boredom. Thoughts and more thoughts come and go; energy is diffused, wasted. You cannot enjoy it; on the contrary, you will be disappointed and disgusted with this unnecessary burden. But the mind, or the intellect, is not at fault. Because an alternative dimension has not been provided, because there is no other door open to it, the energy keeps circling round and round inside you.

Energy can never be stagnant. Energy means that which is not stagnant, that which is always flowing. Relaxation does not mean energy which is stagnant or asleep; scientifically, relaxation means that now energy is flowing through another channel, another dimension—it has entered another room.

But even though the room may be different, if it is not the very opposite of the room you were in before, the mind will not relax. For example, if you work on a scientific problem, then you can relax by reading a novel. The work is different: to deal with a scientific problem is to be active—a very masculine mode whereas to read a novel is to be passive, which is an absolutely feminine mode. Even though you are using the same mind you will be relaxed, because it is the opposite pole of the mind which is being used. You are not solving anything, you are not active, you are just a receiver, receiving something. The dimension is the same except that emotion, the opposite pole, is being brought into use.

In the same way, when we love the intellect does not come into play at all. Quite the opposite happens: the irrational part of your personality comes into action. Intelligence must be balanced by love and love must be balanced by intelligence. Ordinarily, this balance is not found anywhere.

If someone is in love and begins to neglect all intellectual pursuits, this too will create boredom. Even love becomes a tension if it is a twenty-four-hour-a-day affair. Once the challenge is lost, the enjoyment will also be lost: the play will be lost and it will become just work. The same thing happens with an intellectual who neglects the emotional side of his being.

These two parts, these two poles, must be in balance, only then is an integrated and individuated human being born; otherwise, whether emotional or intellectual, it will be the same disease. The East has become warped because it has been too concerned with the heart while the West has been too concerned with the opposite pole. Both have achieved disastrous results.

In the West, the new generation is now rebelling against intellect, against reason—the whole mind of the new generation is leaning toward the irrational. Nature always takes its own revenge. Nature is very vengeful: it never pardons, it never forgets. If some part of it remains suppressed or unfulfilled it will have its revenge. In the West, the irrational is taking its revenge. In the East, the appeal is of the rational, the scientific: communism has much appeal and religion has lost its appeal. The irrational no longer appeals to the East because reason has been suppressed for too long.

To me, neither a human being nor a human culture can be healthy without an inner balance between the rational and the irrational. I do not take them to be two different things. I take them to be two poles of the same energy.

All energy can only exist between two opposite poles, energy requires an inner tension in order to create itself, in order to be. The poles can be negative and positive as in electricity, or north and south as in magnetism, or male and female as in biology, but energy cannot exist at only one pole. The opposite is needed in order to challenge, to stimulate, to create the necessary tension.

But in human society the other pole is always suppressed— either intellect is suppressed or emotion is suppressed. A total culture has not come into existence yet, because there have only been civilizations of either the intellect or of the emotions. Culture, meaning a civilization in which the two poles function simultaneously, is as yet unborn.

Always balance one pole by its opposite. Then the more one pole is put to use, the more the opposite pole for which it is a relaxation will be illuminated. The mind must be capable of changing from one pole to the opposite pole just as easily as one moves from waking to sleeping. One must be able to be close to one dimension and remain open to the other. When this happens life is no longer dull; it becomes bliss.

Unfortunately, we become addicted to one polarity. Why is there this addiction to one extreme? We become addicted to one way of functioning because we have been trained for it. It is easier—you can function in the way that is familiar to you without any conscious effort—consciousness is not required. When you change from one pole to the other, when you change your total perspective, you become an amateur. In this other realm you are not an expert; you are not trained in it. When you try to escape from it, then you tend to overburden that realm in which you are proficient.

This overdoing is the problem. One must not be an expert twenty-four hours a day; one must also do something in which one is a no one and about which one knows nothing. One must be a child sometimes: playing, immature, unknowing, ignorant.

Every genius has a child in him; no genius can exist without a child inside him—this child is the source of all his energy! Because of the child within him, sometimes he can be a novice, sometimes he can be totally ignorant: he can touch realms about which he knows nothing. A mathematician who turns to poetry is never a loser. He comes back to his mathematics with a purer mind, with new experiences that are unknown to mathematics.

Nothing has ever been invented or discovered by someone who is strictly professional. It is always discovered by one who approaches the subject like an outsider coming with the mind of a child. Only a child is inventive, never an old man. The old man is an expert, and an expert cannot invent. He will go on repeating the same thing, doing it and overdoing it; he will make it more perfect but never new. A professional cannot contribute anything new to knowledge because he knows too much, he cannot see the new, he is always oblivious to the new. Professionals are always orthodox, they are never revolutionaries. They cannot be—their very *being* is heavy.

Whenever it happens that a scientist turns to poetry, or a poet turns to mathematics, or a businessman turns to painting, or a painter becomes a *sannyasin*, then something new is born. And to give birth to something new is blissful; otherwise your daily work becomes dull and boring. Man cannot work like a machine—he cannot go on just producing the same things mechanically, repeating the same routine endlessly. If he goes on doing this, he will be completely dead long before he dies. He will only *know* that he has been alive when death comes.

If you are just functioning mechanically as a human machine, there is every danger that you will be replaced by a human-like machine, and you can never be at ease, because whatever you can do can be done more efficiently by a mechanical device.

Society does not need individuality, it needs efficiency. So the more human a person becomes the less useful he is to society—and the more dangerous. The whole pattern of our civilization—and, in fact, of all the civilizations that have existed in the world—is to turn the human being into an automaton. Then he is obedient, efficient—and not dangerous. Otherwise a mind that is inventive, inquiring—seeking and searching for the new and always trying to give birth to something unknown—is bound to create disturbances. The establishment cannot be at ease with him.

Society begins to kill individuality as soon as a child is born. Before he is seven, his individuality is killed completely. Only if by chance the establishment is not successful in doing this can a person become an individual. But this is rare.

Every type of social institution is a means of killing the individual and converting him into a machine. All our universities are factories to kill the spontaneous, to kill the spark, to kill the spirit and change man into a machine. Then the society feels at ease with him. He can be relied upon. The society knows what he can do, what he will do. He can be predicted. We can predict a husband, a wife, a doctor, a lawyer, a scientist. We know who they are and how they will react. We can be at ease with them. But it is impossible to be at ease with a person who is alive, spontaneous, because we don't know what he will do. He is unpredictable.

Unpredictability is always a source of insecurity. A wife cannot be at ease with a husband who is unpredictable. The moment he is unpredictable, he is unmanageable; he cannot be manipulated. No one is at ease with an unpredictable person—not even a father with an unpredictable son!

But only the unpredictable man can feel happiness—can feel like no one else. Life itself is unpredictable, unmanageable. Life as such always moves from moment to moment toward the unknown. It is an opening into the unknown—nothing more, nothing less.

If you are open, just like life itself, then you necessarily live in each of your dimensions: the physical, the intellectual, the emotional, the spiritual. Then you live totally. Then there is no bifurcation, no division; your energy flows as if from one room to another and then to another. There is no barrier to your energy; it is not pulled in any one direction, it is like a flowing river. Then you are always fresh and relaxed. Whenever you return to your particular field of work you approach it with a newness, a freshness that only comes from having relaxed in the opposite dimension.

The problem, as I see it, is not excessive intellectual work but too little or no work in the other dimensions, particularly the emotional. Reason is balanced by emotion. If you can do an exercise in logic but cannot weep, then you are bound to be in trouble. If you can only argue and not laugh, you are inviting trouble.

But whenever a person appears whose life is like a flowing river it is difficult to understand him, because he cannot be categorized.

There is a Zen story:

A famous monk, who was a great teacher, died. He was best known, however, because of his chief disciple. Thousands of people came to pay homage to the monk when he died and to their amazement they found the chief disciple weeping. They were at a loss to understand him. An unattached person should not weep—especially one who has always said that the spirit never dies! Someone came and asked, "Why do you weep?"

The monk replied, "I cannot always live with whys. There are moments when there is no why. I am weeping, that's all."

Still they insisted, "You have always said that the soul is immortal. Why do you weep then?"

He replied, "I still maintain that the soul is immortal. But that does not stop me from weeping."

This sounds illogical: if the soul is immortal, one should not weep. But the monk said, "The soul itself is weeping, and I cannot do anything about it. Whatsoever comes to me, I am one with it. Tears are coming, and I am one with them."

The monk's attitude cannot be categorized. We can understand someone's weeping if he believes that the soul is mortal. If he believes the soul to be immortal and does not weep, that too is understandable, it is all right. The soul is immortal: for whom to weep? No one has died. But the chief disciple had said that the soul is immortal and yet he was weeping. There was no why; the tears were just flowing.

The people asked, "Do you weep for the body?"

The monk said, "Yes, it must be for the body that I am weeping. The body, too, was beautiful and it will never be seen again. I weep for the body."

"But you are a spiritual man," they said. And the argument went on. They accused him of confusing them.

"I myself am confused," he said. "Life is such! The soul is important, but so are my tears. Such is life—so contradictory. It exists in contradictions. I myself am confused; but I am at ease with my confusions, I am at ease with my contradictions, so I am not tense. You see my tears, you see me weeping, but I am at ease. I am relaxed. I am blissful."

The other part must not be denied. The more you use reason, the more you must use the irrational to balance it. The moment it is balanced, you become weightless. You feel free. The weight of one is offset by the weight of the other; a balance is achieved. You are free. Otherwise you will feel the burden, the weight, more and more until a moment comes when nothing exists but the burden. You are no more, only the burden will be felt; that is the only reality you will be conscious of. And the burden will be with you so continuously that you will not be able to conceive of what it is to be without it.

No one is without burden, but one burden can be balanced by another burden from the opposite pole. When the two burdens are balanced, there is no burden. A mind which is not burdened is not really a mind without burdens; rather, it is a mind with *balanced* burdens.

I am in favor of reason and no-reason existing together at the same time. I advise a perpetual balance between the two. As soon as a burden is felt, know that the balance is lost and you must set about restoring it by adding the necessary weight wherever it is required. If the intellect is heavy, do something irrational. Meditate!

Meditation is not concerned with reason; it is irrational. So when someone asks me to explain meditation I am at a loss simply because there is no way that you can "understand" meditation. It is not concerned with logic, reason, arguments, and understanding at all. The only way to know it is to do it.

There are people who have been studying meditation all their lives and still have not understood it. They cannot. Krishnamurti talks about understanding it and makes understanding equivalent to meditation—as if meditation were something to be understood. Rather, understanding must be balanced by meditation, because meditation is the opposite pole, and once you try *not* to understand meditation you can do it.

If one goes on trying to understand meditation, there is less possibility of practicing it. There are people who say that they understand Krishnamurti perfectly. Intellectually, you can understand him, because understanding is intellectual. But even though he says intellectual understanding is not enough, still he equates understanding with meditation.

If intellectual understanding will not do, then only a non-intellectual jump will do. In fact, there is no understanding that is *not* intellectual. Whenever you go into meditation it is less like understanding and more like feeling: it is felt, it is never understood.

Philosophy and science are intellectual processes, religion and art are non-intellectual processes. Philosophy must be balanced by religion and science must be balanced by art; otherwise a topsy-turvy, lopsided world is created in which everyone is diseased.

I have not come across a single individual who is at ease—something or other is always disturbing him. It does not matter what it is, all that matters is that he is disturbed. Everyone is disturbed! There must be something in our very concept of humanity which has gone wrong; something in the very structure of our society has gone wrong. People who are mentally disturbed are only symptomatic of what is happening to the whole society.

There is one very surprising fact: in the 30's, all the mental patients who visited psychoanalysts were primarily disturbed by violence. Then came the Second World War. The same thing had happened in the early twentieth century, and this was followed by the First World War. So as I see it, mental patients are the forerunners of us all: they herald that which is to come. In a way they are more sensitive: they perceive things before the rest of us do.

The same is true of artists. Everything that is to happen first happens in poetry, painting, music, etc. If we look deeply into Picasso's art, for example, we will find the indication of a diseased civilization. In his painting *Guernica*—or, for that matter, in any of his other works—he never portrays a human figure as it is. He never paints all the parts together or puts them in the right context. The head will be in one place, the neck somewhere else, and the eyes may be under the head. Such is his painting: schizophrenic, schizoid. He was an especially sensitive person who saw the shape of things to come, and the plight of the human being in times to come.

A society that is basically only scientific will be lacking in an aesthetic art—art will become ugly. All of Western art has become ugly: grotesqueness and absurdity have become the criteria. Ugliness is appreciated as greatness in art: the more ugly and distorted a painting, the more it is appreciated. There should be no harmony, no rhythm, no music, everything should be deranged and decayed—like the present human mind.

These are indications and symptoms: they are symbolic expressions that the other side of the human mind is taking its revenge; it is demanding attention. A society which is basically only philosophic will be lacking in religion. And when a society becomes less and less religious, religion takes its revenge; it becomes ugly, ritualistic: a church and priesthood emerge and religion diminishes. The church is religion turned ugly, and the priest is the revenge of the prophet. The prophet has no place in the church, so the priest comes in and fills the vacuum.

We have not yet even conceived of a total culture, a total personality, a total mind. The totality is the sum total of the opposite polarities, so a totally consistent personality is an imperfect and partial personality which is, in a way, on the path to madness. This is dangerous. The part that has been denied expression and attention because of a consistent mind will take its revenge. The irrational will become aggressive: it will emerge with a vengeful force and will shatter all reason.

You must not only understand but also feel. It is not difficult to understand intellectually; the problem comes with feeling. You must also *feel!*

This can be possible only when you do something irrational. Jump and dance for an hour and you will see how relaxed and refreshed and alert you will feel. The mind becomes purified because the irrational is satisfied. Now reason can work freely without an enemy waiting to take revenge.

Give both sides of the mind an opportunity to express themselves freely. Always balance the two. Live in these two complementary compartments: the intellect and the emotions. They are not contradictory; they only appear so because we have been living at one extreme and have become fixated there.

When you dream you do not feel the contradiction and inconsistency of the dream. You see a friend approaching, and suddenly he turns into something else. But in the dream you take this as a fact; you feel no inconsistency, no contradiction. You do not ask how a man can change into an animal, because a dream has no logic; it still has to find its Aristotle. In the dream you cannot say that if A is A then it cannot be B; if A is A it cannot be "not A." In the dream, A can be "not A" and "not A" can be A. No logic is taken into account, nor is anything seen to be contradictory. So there are realms that are totally lacking in logic, but which are part of you all the same. Or, it might be better to say that you are part of them, because the fact is that they are greater than you.

When contradictions are not seen to be contradictory, you are never bored. Are you ever bored in a dream? If a balance is achieved between the rational and the irrational, boredom vanishes. There is a moment-to-moment bliss—every moment comes with a bliss of its own. Otherwise life becomes a burden. But life is not responsible for this, we alone are responsible, because the choice lies with us.

SIX

Religion: The Last Luxury

Why is it that Western societies are becoming so interested in Indian religion now?

I consider religion to be the last luxury. Only when a society becomes affluent does religion become meaningful. And now, for the first time, a greater part of the world is not poor—America in particular is the first society in human history to reach such affluence.

To be religious, or to be interested in the ultimate questions of life, one needs to have really fulfilled all the lower wants and needs. So to me, a poor society cannot be religious. India was religious only when it was at a peak of affluence.

For example, in Buddha's time India was just like America is today. In those days, India was the richest land. The religion that we have in India today is just a holdover from those days.

There is a basic difference between a poor man's religion and a rich man's religion. If a poor man becomes interested in religion it will be just as a substitute. Even if he prays to God he will be praying for economic goods; the basic problem of man will not yet have arisen for him. So Marx is right in a way when he says that religion is the opium of the people. He is exactly right about poor people: they cannot get the basic needs of life fulfilled, so they substitute prayer and meditation and yoga and religion. But for a rich man there is a basic change of dimension. Now he is not asking for economic goods, he is asking for the meaning of life.

Krishna, Mahavir, Buddha, the twenty-four *teerthankaras* of the Jains, and the twenty-four *avatars* of the Hindus were all rich people: royally born, sons of kings. India has not had one *avatar* who was a poor man. Only Jesus was poor. That is why he was crucified—a poor man's son can be crucified very easily.

Was he an avatar?

Hindus do not consider him an *avatar*. But then you can consider anyone an *avatar*. Gandhi is considered an *avatar* by Gandhiites, Ramakrishna is considered one by Ramakrishnaites. There are so many *avatars*—but that is not the problem.

The Hindu religion has twenty-four *avatars*; twenty-three have happened and one more is still to come. Buddhists and Jains also have twenty-four Buddhas and *teerthankaras*. All are the sons of kings; none is poor. That is one of the differences between Christianity and Hinduism, Jainism, and Buddhism: Christianity still remains a poor man's religion.

Because of that, Christianity could not achieve higher peaks. If you compare the Hindu scriptures, the Upanishads, with the Bible, the Bible seems poor and childish. The words are the same, the experiences are also the same in a way, but Christianity still remains a religion. Religion—the organized body—and mystical experiences are two different things.

Aren't authentic experiences always the same?

They are, but these spiritual experiences which are the

same are *individual* experiences. The question concerns society, not individual mystics. What I am saying is that a poor man can become a mystic, but a poor society cannot become religious. A rich man is not necessarily religious, but a rich society will become hungry for religion. The moment a society becomes rich, new problems arise. These problems are not concerned with physical bodies and physical needs; they are more psychological.

If a poor man falls ill the illness is more or less concerned with the body. If a rich man falls ill the illness is more or less concerned with the mind. America needs more and more psychologists and psychoanalysis now, because now the greatest number of madmen exist in America. American psychologists say that at least three out of four people are off the rails, not normal.

Your mind's needs arise for the first time when your bodily needs are fulfilled. And religion is a need of the mind, not a body need. That is why animals can live without religion, but man cannot: the mind has come in.

When you are rich, ninety-nine percent of your concern is diverted to the mind. A rich individual may not be religious and a poor individual may be religious, but a poor society as a whole can have religion only as a substitute for economic wealth. Its prayer is not authentic because its prayer tries to demand, to get something.

America is going to become very important and meaningful as far as religion is concerned—America and all the countries that are becoming richer and richer each day. In the coming days, communism will be significant in poor countries and religion will be significant in rich countries. There is no future for religion in poor countries. Within the next twenty years they are all going to turn to communism.

China was a religious country; Russia was a religious country—as religious as any country. And they could wipe out religion in just ten years! China was a Buddhist country: both Taoism and Buddhism were deeply rooted there.

But there, the governments were against religion. That is not likely to happen in India.

That's not the point. Religion, whether the government discourages or encourages it, is not the issue; the *situation* in India is such that religion cannot become meaningful. In a poor country, no matter what shape it takes—you may call it socialism or anything else—communism is going to be the religion. But in Russia religion will again become meaningful in twenty years' time. Russia is not a poor country now and the moment a society becomes rich, you cannot escape religion. It is impossible.

Is it right to delegate religion only to the rich?

It is not a question of right and wrong for me, it is a question of what the correct situation is. A person who is ill will go to the hospital and a person who is not ill will not go. So a poor country is bound to be attracted by communism. That is just the flow of history—in a way it is inevitable. In the same way a rich country is bound to be attracted by religion.

In Russia, things have changed within the last ten or fifteen years. Now they have the greatest number of research scientists working on research projects in parapsychology in the whole world. And their findings are miraculous!

So it is not a question of right and wrong, it is just the way that history moves. In the long run communism does bring a certain affluence; then religion can become meaningful.

Is this due to the human need for newness?

It is only the young man who becomes interested in new things. An old man has such an investment in old things that he cannot be interested in new things. And it is always the youth who feels the future in his veins, not the old man. The past is the home of the old man, the future that of the young man. Because the young man will be living in the future, he is more interested in new developments, in new things.

The young are always dissatisfied—always. Dissatisfaction is in their very hearts; otherwise they could not be young. If romance were absolutely satisfied they would not just be old but already dead. They always feel a discontent, a dissatisfaction, an inner restlessness. It is a good sign. Because of the inner restlessness they are ready to move into new dimensions.

Why are young people so rebellious nowadays?

There are many factors. One is universal education: for the first time the youth of the world are well-educated. And to the educated mind the old establishment looks absurd and out of date—rooted in the past, of course, but with no future.

Secondly, the scientific progress of the world and the scientific training of the young basically presupposes a training in doubt. Since all the old cultures and civilizations are based on faith, there is a gap. The young are trained for doubt and all religions and cultures require faith, so it becomes impossible. The young are now really in search of a faith which can be scientific: a faith which is so alive that it can allow doubt, a faith that is unafraid of doubt.

Life is complex, and everything exists with its polar opposite. A scientist begins with doubt and ends in faith while a religious man—the religious man of old—begins with faith. That is the only difference. And, as I see it, the faith that begins with doubt is deeper, because it is unafraid of doubt.

Doubt is not against faith, it is a way *toward* faith; it can be used as an instrument. If you can doubt rightly, you will come upon faith. And then your faith will be well grounded; it will not be a blind belief.

Thirdly, the world has become one: it has come so much closer together that local traditions cannot continue now. We need one culture, one civilization, and what we have are many cultures, many civilizations. And that creates confusion.

Once, everyone was enclosed in his own local world. A Hindu was a Hindu, with no awareness of anything else. It was impossible to conceive that anything else could be an alternate path. But now we are acquainted with multi-alternatives; the world has become an open world. No one is rooted in his local culture now, and that creates restlessness. In a way, we are uprooted. We have to build a world culture.

But before a world culture can come into being, local cultures will have to die. That is why the youth of today appear to be rebellious. It is not really the young who are rebellious, it is the resistance of the old establishment to the new world which creates rebelliousness.

Fourthly, we have created atomic weapons for the first time. Now there are two alternatives: either we will have to learn to live together or we will die together—universal suicide or a universal society. Because of the possibility of total atomic war, the young are restless. The future is blurred. There seems to be no future—an atomic war can happen at any moment, there may be no time to live—so this very moment becomes very meaningful.

There is a deep correlation between time-consciousness and restlessness: the more time-conscious a society is, the more restless it becomes. But a society is always contented if it has no time-consciousness. In the East, we have lived very contented lives for centuries only because of the theory of reincarnation: "Time is infinite. If this life is lost, nothing is lost." But for Christianity there is only life: "Time is very short and man has much living to do." Time is so short that one becomes restless.

With atomic war threatening, there is no more time left for the future: it seems that any day the whole planet may be destroyed. For the first time, youth is more concerned with the present moment—to live it, to enjoy it—because there seems to be no future.

So these are the causes. But to me, they are all good signs because through them we can create a new world and a new human mind can be born. The hippie slogan is good: "Make love not war." It is good! After 1984 either there is going to be no world or an absolutely different world. And I hope for the latter.

Why are most meditation methods not more fruitful in helping people?

There are many meditation methods and each method is meaningful to a particular type of mind. Then, too, there are certain methods that are meaningful in a particular age.

All of our traditional methods are basically silent ones. My method of Dynamic Meditation ends in silence but begins in catharsis because in our age our minds need a deep catharsis first; only then can they become silent.

This method is needed only because the modern mind—whether Christian or non-Christian, Hindu or non-Hindu—is a by-product of a very suppressive attitude toward desires, thoughts, instincts—everything. We have lived for centuries with a very repressive attitude toward life. That repression has to be thrown out first, only then can you enter your center.

So my method is new in a way—not in its results but only in the methodology. First you must throw your madness out; only then can you enter the inner.

What is your concept of sannyas?

My concept of *sannyas* is totally different or, rather, totally contrary to the old concept of *sannyas*. The old concept of *sannyas* is one of withdrawing oneself from the world. My concept is that of just taking an inner attitude without any outward withdrawal. You remain in the world, you go on working as you were working, but now you are not serious about it. Now it is just an act. You are in the middle of a drama, that's all.

There is no need to withdraw—I discourage any withdrawal because if you are not seriously involved in the world, you can be in it and above it.

So be in the world but do not allow the world to be in you. That is *sannyas*.

SEVEN

Secrets of Discipleship

What is the guru/disciple relationship?

First of all, a guru is *not* a teacher; a guru is a person who has attained to a religious mode of living. Religion is not information, it cannot be taught because religion is a way of living. The very presence of the guru is a communion. And to one living in contact with him, something is communicated—though not through words. The relationship is so intimate that it is less like teacher and pupil and more like lover and beloved.

The guru must himself be enlightened, he must himself have attained, because one cannot communicate that which one has not realized. Religious experience can be communicated only when it is first-hand. A teacher need not be self-realized, but a guru must be. A teacher can give second-hand information from scriptures or traditions, but a guru cannot; a guru is a person who has realized truth. Now *he* is the original source—he himself has encountered reality, he is face to face with it—and the disciple comes in contact with a first-hand knowing because whatsoever is said or communicated to him by the guru is on his own authority.

Secondly, a guru is not aware of his guruship; he cannot be. A guru cannot claim that he is a guru—there is no claim like that. A person can only *know* whether or not he has fulfilled the condition of egolessness; otherwise he cannot encounter truth. Truth is encountered only when the ego is absolutely absent.

I always say that in religion, in spirituality, *only disciples exist*—because the guru is not present, he is only a presence. His very non-claiming, his non-egoistic, non-teaching attitude, and his living the truth, are the communion. So a person who claims to be a guru is only a teacher, he is not a guru.

There is no word in English to translate the word "guru" because the relationship between guru and disciple is basically Eastern. No such relationship has ever existed in Western culture and tradition, so no one in the West can understand what a guru is. At most they can understand what a teacher is.

The relationship between guru and disciple is so intimate . . . it is like love. The reverence that is felt is like love but with one difference: love is parallel and reverence is for one who is above, one who is higher. Love creates friendship because the lover and the loved one are on the same level. Reverence too is a kind of love but with a great difference: it is not on the same level; one person is higher. If there is a loving intimacy with the higher personality, reverence is automatically created around a guru. But it is not expected, it is not demanded.

Only disciples exist—because they are *consciously* disciples, they *choose* to be disciples. A guru does not choose, he acts—the action is one with his living so that he teaches by his very act. His teaching and his living are two aspects of a single existence: his very sitting, standing, walking, his talking, his silence—everything is an indication. Something happens through the guru's very existence and the disciple always has to be ready to receive it. "Disciple" means one who has an open mind, a receptive mind so he is not just learning but receiving. That is why trust is a basic component of being a disciple.

Whenever we are confronted with the unknown, no logic, no rational explanation is possible. Whenever we are confronted with the unknown, only trust can lead us. If I say something about the known then you can discuss it with me because you also know it. We can argue about it, we can talk about it—a dialogue is possible. But if I talk about something that is absolutely unknown to you, then no dialogue is possible and there can be no argument. There can be no rational approach to it because reason can only work around the known.

The moment the unknown comes in, reason is useless: it becomes meaningless. Thinking is absurd because you cannot think about the unknown. It is just as if you are blind and I talk to you about light. You can only take what I say on trust; there is no other way.

The relationship between the disciple and the guru is a relationship of intimate trust. That doesn't mean blind faith, because the guru never expects you to believe in him. That is not an expectation! But the very nature of the unknown is such that you cannot go a single step further without trust. Trust is required of the disciple because he will not be able to take a single step into the unknown without trusting the guru. The unknown is dark, the field is uncharted—it is not bliss, it is not the ultimate—and the guru is always saying "Jump into it! Do it!" But before you can jump, trust is needed or you will not jump. And knowledge can only come through a jump.

In science, a hypothesis is needed before there can be an experiment. "Hypothesis" means a tentative belief. If the experiment proves the hypothesis then it becomes a truth, but if the experiment disproves it, it becomes an untruth. But without a hypothesis, a tentative belief, there can be no experiment.

It is exactly the same with religion: trust is needed just as a hypothesis is needed in science. But there is a great difference between a scientific attitude and a trustful attitude. A person can believe hypothetically in a scientific proposition and yet be skeptical about it. Reverence is not needed because it concerns an objective phenomenon: you can experiment with it and see how it turns out. But in religion, a hypothetical belief is not enough because you are not tackling an objective problem that is outside you. You are tackling yourself; it is a subjective phenomenon. You will have to be involved, committed. You will not be doing the experiment from outside, you will *be* the experiment: you will have to jump in and become part of it. Great trust is needed.

So the relationship between guru and disciple is one of great trust, intimate love, reverence. But these things are not demanded. The moment they are demanded they become exploitation; the moment they are forced they become violent, because no one should force himself on anybody. It is not an enforcement on the part of the guru, it is a willingness on the part of the disciple to allow the guru to work.

But ordinarily, the disciple is unwilling and the guru is forcing. Then everything becomes nonsense. The moment the guru tries to force something on someone, it cripples, it destroys, it kills, because it is a violent act against someone else's ego. But if the disciple is willing, if he gives the guru his complete trust—if it is not forced, if it is his own willing surrender—then a great transformation happens: the disciple is transformed by his very surrender.

This is a very decisive act: to surrender oneself to someone else completely, totally. It is not just faith in someone else, it is basically faith in oneself. You cannot surrender yourself if you are not confident enough about your decision, because it is a great decision—total and unconditional. Whenever a disciple surrenders himself his will is involved, and out of his will a decision is born. The disciple becomes a crystallized personality through surrender because the decision is so great and so total, so absolute and unconditional.

No surrender can be conditional; there can be no condition with the guru. You cannot say, "If you do this then I will surrender." Then it will not be surrender. There is no *if*—you surrender totally. You say, "Do whatsoever you like. I am in your hands. Ask me to jump into a wall, and I will jump!"

This very decision to surrender totally is transforming and crystallizing. The attitude of the disciple is always one of total surrender. Then the guru is able to do anything because, through your total receptivity to him, you can be in communion with him. Then, by and by, you change.

The matter is delicate, it is very sensitive: to change a living being, to change a human personality, is the greatest, most arduous, most delicate thing. The human personality is so complex, it is in so much conflict, with so much that is suppressed and perverted, that to change it and to make it flower in ecstasy, to make it a worthy present for the divine, is the greatest art or science possible.

But you must remember that what I have been talking about always comes from the disciple, never from the guru. If it comes from the guru then Krishnamurti is right: then gurudom is one of the most subtle and destructive exploitations. But Krishnamurti is not right really, because surrender has never been a demand of the guru; it is a basic condition for discipleship. Without the guru or a relationship of trust, it is very difficult to progress spiritually. In fact, it is not possible.

There is every possibility that a person may flower without any guru, but that person too will have to surrender, he will have to trust—if not a particular person then the whole. The basic requirements must be fulfilled. Whether they are fulfilled in connection with a person or not is immaterial.

It is easier to trust a person than to trust the whole. If you cannot trust a person you can never trust existence as such. If you cannot surrender in a personal relationship, you can never surrender to the impersonal divine. So the guru is a step toward the impersonal, a way to help one toward surrender to the whole, to existence itself.

To the human mind, all relationships are personal. It may be love, it may be respect, it may be anything, but it is personal. So the first step toward the realization of truth or of cosmic being is also bound to be personal. Someone will have to be used as a jumping board.

And there are other things also.

Words cannot communicate much that is meaningful as

far as spirituality is concerned. The very phenomenon is such that it is inexpressible. If you hear some instrumental music, you cannot convey the meaning of it through words. You can use judgmental words—"good," "bad"—but they do not convey anything. You can only convey your feelings, and those too, very inadequately.

If you have seen a flower, you can say it is beautiful. But that does not convey anything. Your words never convey the actual realization of the moment because they can mean anything to the person to whom they are conveyed. A person who has never seen beauty in any flower will hear your words and understand the meaning of them without understanding anything at all, because the word "beauty" does not mean anything to him.

Even concepts such as beauty are not totally expressible—we can only *try* to express them. Spiritual things are so impeccable, so silent, so infinite, that language destroys them. Words confine them to such a narrow sphere that the meaning cannot be conveyed. That is why I said that religion cannot be taught.

However difficult, mathematics can be taught because it is symbolic, and symbols can be conveyed. Physics can be taught because there is nothing inexpressible about it. But the nearer you come to the human heart—for example, in poetry—the more you feel that your words have not conveyed the thing, that something has been left behind. The container is there, but the content has been left behind. The words have reached, but the meaning has been left behind. The flower has been received, but the perfume has died in the very giving of it.

Words are at the mid-point between science and religion: in science everything can be conveyed; in religion nothing can be conveyed. These are the three roads: science, which means reason, and is expressible; poetry and art, which are emotion, and are expressible up to a certain point beyond which they become inexpressible; and religion, spirituality, which is absolutely inexpressible.

That is why the relationship between guru and disciple is not that of teacher and pupil. Religion cannot be taught.

Then how is it conveyed? There are other methods.

When you are in love with someone, gestures become meaningful for the first time. A slight twinge in the face is detected, a slight waver in the eyes is known and understood. Unless you are in love you never pay attention to such minute things; you just see a face but you don't see its total complexity, you don't see its constantly changing patterns. You see the face as an external thing, you never see the content in it. But when you love someone the face is not just a figure but a living pattern. Minute things and subtle changes in expression are detected and known. Even before the lover has said something, you have known it. Even before the lover comes to know that he has felt something, you can detect it.

And reverence is even more subtle than love. The very *existence* of the guru is a communication: everything that he is constantly delivers messages which are caught, known, decoded, and understood by the reverent mind. These gestures, these living gestures, are a language.

The communication is even deeper when the relationship becomes ripe. When the disciple has blossomed into disciplehood and he understands completely the meaning of his guru's words and gestures, he is ripe. Then a silent communication, without gestures, without any linguistic symbols, is possible. This telepathic communication is the secret of the relationship: it is the most secret key of communion between guru and disciple. Only when this becomes possible has the disciple been accepted. Then there is no question of time and space. Then, wherever the disciple is, things can be communicated to him.

All these things have to be waited for patiently. It is a great waiting. You can never be in a hurry as far as spiritual learning is concerned because a hurried mind cannot go so deep, it cannot be so silent. The disciple should not be in a hurry to know, he should await the right moment: trusting, waiting, and preparing himself.

In the West they can never understand why a disciple should serve the guru. "Why should he be a servant?" They do not know that service is a way of communion. When a disciple serves a guru, when he waits and serves, the division drops—he becomes one with the guru. The guru's body and his own body are not two things now. He feels the pain of the guru, the illness of the guru. He feels the pleasure of the guru, the ecstasy of the guru. By and by, he becomes totally absorbed in the guru. Through this absorption with the guru's body he becomes one with the guru. You cannot become one spiritually if you cannot become intimate and one with the body; the body is the base.

The disciple goes on serving the guru and never asks any questions. This is a miracle! He will not say, "Teach me this or that," because even to say this is to mistrust the guru. When the moment is right he will be told. When the moment is right he will be taught. If the moment is not right he will just wait. Sometimes he will wait for years—even today. Twenty years may pass and he will just be waiting. He may have gone as a youth and now he is an old man—but still he is waiting! This very waiting, this patience, creates a situation in which the guru and the disciple are not two; they are one. The moment they become one, what is not expressible can be expressed.

Wittgenstein has said somewhere that what cannot be said can be shown. Saying needs no patience, but showing needs much patience. If I want to say something to you, I can say it this very moment. Your patience, your preparation is not needed. I can say it, and you will hear it. But if I want to show you something then you will have to make great preparations in order to *see* it. I cannot show it to you unless you have the capacity to see.

The guru is basically not saying anything but trying to show something, and if the disciple is aware, then things become clear by not intervening. Things are always clear, but the mind is confused—and a confused mind confuses things. As far as worldly things are concerned your mind cannot distort them too much because they are so objective that they do not depend on your mind. But the spiritual is so subjective, it depends so much on your vision, that a confused mind can misunderstand and destroy everything.

Destruction comes from our past accumulated knowledge. The mind has known and accumulated so much that it comes in and muddles everything; the old has come in between.

What you come to know must not be interpreted! Everything that is new must be seen with a new mind. If one can put this knowledge aside and see into things directly, immediately, then things are always clear. Existence is so innocently pure and clear—everything is so crystal clear—that it is a miracle how the human mind confuses it. This confusion comes through interpretation; it comes from using all that is known to understand that which is not known.

If we can be totally aware of anything new that is presented to us, if we can become receptive and aware of its presence, then it goes directly to the heart. What I am saying may appear irrational, but it is the truth. The mind never understands; only the heart understands. The center of understanding is never the mind, it is always the heart. The heart is always pure, fresh, and virgin; it is never burdened by the past. But the mind is never virgin, it is never new; it is always old. It is always of the past, it is always of the dead—an accumulation of dead experiences. So whenever the mind is working, you always misunderstand. You are bound to. But when it is not working—when it is quiet, silent, absolutely non-existent, when only awareness is there—a gap is created and the door to the heart is opened.

The heart understands without any interpretation; its understanding is direct and immediate. You just understand—you *know*. "This is so." This putting the mind aside is what I call meditation. If you can see things through the heart, if you can contact existence through the heart, then you are in meditation. But if you are always living through the mind you will never be in meditation.

It can be said that the heart is the faculty for meditation

and the mind is the faculty which functions against meditation. And the two cannot work simultaneously: if the mind is
functioning, the heart cannot. It goes away because it is not
needed; it goes to sleep. Only when the mind is not working
does the heart come to the surface to breathe, to see. It comes
only when the mind is not needed, when the mind has been
discarded. And the moment the heart comes in contact with
the existential, you feel the ecstasy, the beatitude. Everything
becomes divine. It *is* divine, but then you know it.

When the heart is in contact with the world, the world is
divine. When the mind is in contact with the world, the
world is material. Mind cannot know anything beyond matter and the heart cannot know anything below the spiritual.
That is why those who have been heart-oriented have said
that the world is unreal, illusory: it is *maya*—just a magical
show. There is a reason for saying so. Because the heart cannot come below the spiritual, it can never know the material.
The material world becomes illusory, unreal, dreamy—as if it
were not.

The mind-oriented have denied the spiritual. They say
that it is a dream, fiction which is nowhere to be found. Only
matter exists for them. There is nothing spiritual: the spiritual
is illusory, dream-like, foolish. Nietzsche has said somewhere,
"There are people who say that Jesus was a genius, a wise
man. But I would like to say that he was an idiot!" To a
person looking at existence through the mind, everything of
the heart seems idiotic.

The East has been heart-oriented; the West has been
mind-oriented. The Western mind has been able to create a
great scientific edifice but the Eastern mind could not—how
can you create a science from innocence? It is impossible. So
the East has been living unscientifically.

But the West has never been able to know what meditation is. At the most they could pray. But to pray is not the
point. You can only pray *with the mind*; you can go on repeating formulas. If there is no mind, prayer will be silent: you will

not be able to pray—there will be no words. With the heart you can only be *prayerful*.

In the West they could not develop a spiritual science, they could not develop meditation. They converted meditation into either concentration or contemplation—it is neither—and thereby missed the point. Concentration is a mental process. When the mind is concentrated and the whole thought process is focused, it becomes thinking. It is not a question of the heart.

Meditation is neither contemplation nor concentration. It is a non-mental, no-mind living. It is to be in contact with the world with no mind in between. The moment mind is absent, there is no barrier between you and existence, between you and the divine, because the heart cannot draw boundaries, it cannot define. By defining things, the mind creates barriers, boundaries, frontiers. But with the heart, existence becomes frontierless. You end nowhere, and no one else begins anywhere. You are everywhere, one with the whole of existence.

The heart cannot feel duality—duality is a mental creation. The mind divides, analyzes; it cannot work without division. That is why science goes on analyzing molecules, atoms, electrons: dividing existence into smaller and smaller parts. The more divisions there are, the more the mind is at ease, because then existence becomes more defined; it can be manipulated, it can be easily known. But the vaster it is, the greater and more infinite existence becomes, the more the mind feels awe. It cannot define it: existence becomes mysterious.

The scientific method of tackling a mystery is analysis—analyze a thing and solve the mystery. If the whole world could be analyzed there would be no mystery. But the mystery remains unsolved, because to solve it requires synthesis.

Drop all definitions, drop all boundaries, and everything becomes mysterious. Then you are one with the mystery: then everything is divine. That is the only solution and the only way to know existence. Let scientific definitions drop, and a world without definitions, without boundaries, comes into existence: a synthesized whole, an organic unity, a crystallized oneness. This oneness—the feeling of it, the knowing of it, and the living of it—is what I mean by God.

Meditation is the way to know God. Mind is the way to know matter. Mind and meditation are exact opposites—different dimensions. You cannot have it both ways. You can reach the mind, but in that moment the heart will not work. You can reach the heart, but in that moment the mind will not work. You can use both, but not simultaneously; they are polar opposites.

Without meditation, everything is rational and yet absurd, because it is meaningless. With meditation, everything is irrational but meaningful. And the moment life is meaningful, life *is*. When it is not meaningful, when it is rationally understood but meaningless, then it is not. It is as dead as can be. This is the paradox: with the mind, you can understand but the moment is lost; with the heart, you cannot understand but the meaning is known, felt, realized.

With the mind, everything can be categorized and manipulated, but you are nullified through it and in the end there is no mystery. Once the mind has understood everything, nothing remains but suicide, because no one can live without mystery. The more life is a mystery, the more it is worth living.

Religion is knowing the mystery and still not destroying it. The religious way of knowing is very different—it is neither logical nor rational; it is absolutely fresh. But our minds become uneasy with it because we are so obsessed with reason; this very minute part of the mind, reason, has become our sum total, our "all."

Life is not rational; it is basically irrational—and this *irrationality* of life and existence is the mystery. If everything becomes mysterious to you, then you are here and now in the divine. With meditation, the mystery is revived: you again come in contact with the mysterious.

Meditation is of the heart, and the heart has its own methods of understanding which are absolutely different from reason, absolutely different from the mind. I would like all of you to know more of the heart.

The guru/disciple relationship is an understanding of the heart. The East has so many secret keys, but even a single key is enough because a single key can open thousands and thousands of locks. The relationship between guru and disciple is one such key.

EIGHT

God Is
Existence Itself

Does God exist? How can there be so much
evil and corruption in the world if God exists?

"God" is a mythical word, a mumbo-jumbo word that is
the invention of the priesthood. Actually, to ask whether God
exists in absurd. For those who know, God is existence, or
existence is God.

Things exist, not God. A chair exists because a chair can
go into non-existence. To say that the chair exists is meaningful because its non-existence is possible.

God *is* existence, the very is-ness. When we say "God exists" we create something out of the word "God": then God
becomes a thing. But God is not a thing, nor is God a person.
That is why you cannot make him responsible for anything.
Responsibility only comes when there is a personality, when
there is someone who can be responsible.

God is not a person; he is pure existence. The word is
misleading because the word personifies. It is better to use the
word "existence." The totality of existence is God.

So it cannot be asked whether God exists. That is like
asking whether existence exists. Put this way—whether existence exists—the question becomes absurd. Obviously existence exists; there is no question about it. The question
cannot even exist if there is no existence, nor can the questioner.

I would like to make it clear that when I say "God," I mean existence as such. God is not a thing among other things, God is total thing-ness. To say that the table exists is the same as saying that the table is God. To say that you exist is the same as saying that you are God. God is the existence, God is is-ness: the quality of is-ness, the quality of existence.

First of all, God is not a thing. Secondly, God is not a person, because the total cannot be a person. Personality is a relationship. Alone, totally alone, you will not be a person at all, you will be existence itself. That is why those who are seeking the divine tend to go into loneliness. In this way, they can cease to be persons and can become one with existence. Loneliness, absolute loneliness, is a step toward jumping into the abyss of existence.

God is not a person because there is nothing opposite to him, nothing distinct from him. God cannot say "I" because there is no other that exists as "thou." He cannot be related to anyone. He is the whole, so all relationships exist in him and cannot exist beyond him.

So if God is not a person, there is no question of any responsibility. If evil exists, it exists. No one is responsible for it. The total cannot be responsible for it.

Responsibility implies that there is a person who can be responsible. A child of four cannot be taken to court because he is not yet a person and therefore cannot be held responsible for anything that he may have done. He is so innocent that even the sense of personality, the sense of ego, is not there. He is not responsible at all, because responsibility comes with ego. Existence has no ego at all—God has no ego at all—so you cannot make him responsible for any evil that exists.

But the human mind is very cunning. First we invent a personified God—we give God a personality—and then we make him responsible for what happens. We go on creating problems that are not problems at all but only linguistic fallacies. Ninety-nine percent of philosophy consists only of linguistic fallacies. If you call the totality "existence" you cannot make it responsible; but if you call it "God," then you can make it responsible. Only the word has changed.

"Existence" is non-personal, impersonal. But if "God" becomes a person, then you can ask, "Why is there evil?" The whole game is being played by you alone; God is not a party to it. When you give existence a name, a personal name, you create problems. These problems are not authentic problems; they are created problems, invented problems.

"God" means existence. I cannot say that God exists, because that would be a tautology. It would be just like saying: existence exists, or poetry is poetry. It means nothing, it defines nothing, it clarifies nothing, it explains nothing; it only repeats itself.

To me, God is existence, and existence is impersonal. It cannot be otherwise because the total cannot be a person. How can it be? In contrast to whom can it be an individual, a person? In contrast to whose ego can it create its own ego?

You become an ego because other egos exist. Psychologists say that the sense of ego develops in a child later than the sense of the other. First the child becomes aware of others, then he becomes aware of himself. The ego is a later addition.

You cannot become aware of yourself if there is no "other." Without the other you cannot define yourself—your definition of yourself comes from the other. Others define you; they make you separate. By knowing others you come to feel your own boundaries. Then you know, "I am here, and I am not there." Then you know, "This body is mine, and that body is not mine." Then what is you is clearly defined— defined by other egos. If there were no "other," you would never be aware of yourself as a person.

God cannot become an ego. He cannot say "I" because there is no "thou": he cannot define himself. God is indefinable because a definition means a drawing of boundaries, and the total has no boundaries at all, the total means that which has no boundaries, the infinite.

We cannot conceive of the infinite—whatsoever is conceivable by the mind is finite. Even when we think about the infinite we conceive of it as a greater finiteness, never as the infinite. We cannot conceive of a boundary-less existence, but it is so nevertheless. Whether you can conceive of it or not makes no difference.

Mind cannot conceive of the indefinable, because mind requires definitions, clear-cut boundaries. That is why God, existence, cannot be understood by the mind.

God is the indefinable. Because we use the pronoun "he" for a person, we use "he" for God. But "he" is not correct, because by calling God "he," he becomes a person. Still, there is no other way. If we call God "it," it may seem better, but since we call things "it," God also becomes a thing. Our language is not meant to express the indefinable, so the best we can do is use "he." But he is not a person at all, he is a no-person, a non-ego. You cannot make him responsible.

If you say that something is bad—that there is evil or there is want—you are saying it to no one. No reply will be given to you from the universe, because as far as existence itself is concerned there *is* no evil. Evil depends on our attitudes; it depends on our moralistic definitions. For example, you may call someone ugly, but there is no ugliness in existence itself because there is no beauty. The distinction is human, it is not existential. You have made the definition: you have defined something as beauty and something else as ugliness. You have made the distinction and then you ask, "Why has God made ugliness?"

There is no way to decide what is good and what is bad. If there were no human beings on earth, would there be anything good or bad? There would be no good and no bad because goodness and badness are human distinctions, mental distinctions. If there were no human beings on earth would there be any flower that was ugly or any flower that was beautiful? There would only be flowers flowering; the distinction would not be there.

You say "this is evil" and "that is good." But if, for example, Adolf Hitler's mother had killed him during his childhood, would it have been good or bad? She would have been a criminal and they would have punished her for it. But now, looking back, we can say that it would have been a most moral act: by killing her child, she could have saved the whole world.

No one can know the future. For us, every act is an incomplete act, every act is a fragment. We don't know the whole so we cannot pronounce judgment on it.

It is just like a page torn from a novel—how can you make any judgment about the novel by reading just one page? You don't know anything about the novel, this is just a fragment—it has no beginning or end. You will say, "I would like to read the whole story first. Nothing can be said about it otherwise. This page is not enough."

Words such as "good" and "bad" are just expedient, utilitarian; they are not existential. We cannot exist without classifying things as either good or bad because otherwise society would be impossible.

This must be clearly understood. Definitions are not ultimate truths, they are relative. There is not a single act that cannot be considered good in some context. A good deed can be bad in one context and a bad deed may be good in another. If you are to make any final judgment you will have to know everything from the very beginning to the very end—everything in the whole of existence. But of course, this is impossible.

All our statements about good and bad, beauty and ugliness, are nothing more than traffic regulations. We have to make them, but they are not ultimate truths. "Keep left" or "keep right"—it makes no difference. But no society can do both: either you have to keep right or you have to keep left. The rule is utilitarian; it is neither natural nor ultimate.

The road is absolutely unconcerned with whether you keep to the right or to the left, but traffic does require certain rules. When there is less traffic you do not have to make any rules; but the more confusing the traffic, the more rules will be needed. In a village there is no need for traffic rules, but in a big city rules are needed.

As society develops in a more complex way, a more clearly defined morality is needed; otherwise you will not be able to live. But these moralities, these conceptions of good and bad, are human expediencies.

When you ask how there can be corruption if God exists, remember: God is not involved at all. There are reasons for corruption, but God is not responsible, the total is not responsible. If responsibility is to be put anywhere, it is to be put on us. We have created a society in which corruption has become necessary because its very base is corrupt.

Unless you change the very foundation of society there is bound to be corruption; there has always been corruption. Forms have changed, but the corruption has remained because we have not yet created a society in which corruption is impossible.

This situation is our creation; God is not involved in it at all. It is as much a human creation as this table, this sofa, this house. You cannot hold God responsible for this house, or for this room's being small and not large, or for this window's facing west and not east. You never ask God, "Why did you build this window onto the east wall and not the west?" That would be nonsense—you know that it is some person who built the window into the east wall. God has never been asked about it, he is not a party to it.

In the same way you can ask why there is corruption, but you cannot make any reference to God. To ask why there is corruption is a pertinent question. But to talk about God in reference to corruption is impertinent. Our society has been made by *us*—we are the architects of it. And because the foundation of it is wrong, because the base upon which we have built all of society's structures is not scientific, it is bound to be corrupt. It is a human problem. We can change it or we can prolong it—it depends on us.

For example, our whole education is ambition-oriented. Our whole society is ambitious and an ambitious society can never be anything but corrupt. If you create ambition in everyone, not everyone will be able to fulfill it. You may say that anyone can be president, but only one person can be president at any one time. When you teach that everyone can be president, ambition is created: if *everyone* can be president then why shouldn't you be? But since only one person can be president, a mad rush begins. Every means will be used—even evil means will be used.

Ambition corrupts: the ambitious mind is bound to be corrupt. Ambition is the seed of insanity. Yet our whole education is ambition-oriented. Your father says, "Become someone!" and the fever is created—you become diseased. Only one person can be president, and thousands of people who will be unsuccessful are aflame with the same ambition. Then you cannot be sane—you become insane. Because so much tension is created you become corrupt: you will use any means to achieve your goal.

It is infectious. If you see that someone else is using corrupt means you know that if you don't use them you will be left behind. So you have to use equally corrupt means. Then someone else sees you being unscrupulous, so he has to be unscrupulous. It becomes a question of survival. Nothing else is possible within this framework, this structure. If you look to the very roots of society you will see that corruption is a natural outgrowth of our conditioning, our education, our cultivation.

The complexity of our social structure is such that those who succeed can hide their corruption. Corruption is seen only when someone fails. If you succeed no one will know that you have been corrupt; success will hide everything. You have only to succeed and you will become a pinnacle of goodness—you will become everything that is good, pure, innocent. That means you can succeed in any way you like, but you *must* succeed. Once you succeed, once you are successful, nothing that you may have done is wrong.

This has been true throughout history. A person is only a thief if he is a small thief. If he is a great thief, then he becomes an Alexander the Great, a hero. No one ever sees that there is no qualitative difference between the two, that it is only a quantitative difference. No one will call Alexander the Great a great thief because the measure of your "goodness" is success: the more successful you are, the more "good." Means are only questioned if you are a failure; then you will be called both corrupt and a fool.

If this is the attitude, how is it possible to create an uncorrupt society? To ask a person to be moral in this immoral situation is to ask something absurd. An individual cannot be moral in an immoral society—if he tries to be moral, his morality will only make him egoistic. And ego is as immoral and corrupt as anything else.

This situation is a human creation. We have created a society with a mad rush for wealth, power, politics; we go on supporting it, and then we ask why there is corruption. Where there is ambition, corruption will be the logical consequence. You cannot check corruption unless the whole basic structure that encourages ambition is destroyed.

Ambition even becomes manifest around a so-called saint. He will incite you to ambition in terms of comparison; he will say, "Become better than others. Be good so that you will go to heaven and be the beloved of the divine while others will be tortured in the fires of hell." The poison of ambition can easily be used in order to make a person "good."

But that is not really possible. A person may be ambitious and bad—that is natural, logical—but he cannot be ambitious and good. It is impossible. If a person wants to be good, he cannot think in terms of comparison, because the flowering of real goodness only comes when there is no comparison.

Comparison is the barrier because comparison creates ego, it creates violence. The moment you say, "I am more humble than you," you have become violent. You have used a subtle, cunning method that thrusts a knife into the other; you have killed him. The weapon is lethal—and much more subtle than political or capitalist weapons. If you say, "I am better than others, I am more saintly than others," then the object may be different, but you will be on the same ambitious track. Criminals and sinners are not the only ones who are corrupt;

the so-called good people, the "saints," are also corrupt—in a more subtle way.

Our whole society is corrupt: it creates sinners with ambition and saints with ambition. And they are interdependent, because both exist on the same axis: the axis of ambition. A person who understands this will drop out of society completely. He will be neither a sinner nor a saint—he will not fit himself into *any* category—and you will be at a loss to measure who he is, what kind of a person he is. We need a society that is non-ambitious.

God is not involved in it at all, but if you are ambitious, even God will become part of your ambition. You will pursue him, you will try to attain to God.

A person who is ambitious is never able to attain to God. He is never relaxed, he is never loving—because ambition is violence. And a person who is not at ease, who is not loving, who is not silent or peaceful, can never know what God is. God is not something that can be known intellectually; he is something that can only be felt.

When you are at ease, totally relaxed, going nowhere—when the mind is still and at peace with itself—then you know what existence is. Then you know the beauty and the bliss of existence. It is not beauty in contrast to ugliness; there is no contrast and there is no comparison. Rather, everything becomes beautiful—the very existence is beautiful. Then a cactus is as beautiful as a rose. Then individuality is beautiful; it is incomparable.

Then for the first time you begin to love. It is not a love that exists in contrast to hate because that kind of "love" can never really be love, it is bound to be a diluted form of hate, a non-intense form of hate. It is the opposite pole: love exists at one pole and hate exists at the other pole, and you go on wavering between the two. Your hate means less love. Your love means less hate.

You may ask how one can be beyond hate and love. You can only be beyond the duality of love and hate if you are no longer ambitious, if you are no longer tense, if you are relaxed.

Going nowhere, seeking nothing at all. Just being. Then you know God and, simultaneously, you know love. Love is a by-product of being in tune with the infinite; it follows just like a shadow; it is a consequence.

Buddha never searched for love; love just came to him. Jesus never thought about love, he lived love. The search for love cannot be direct—it is such a subtle perfume that you cannot search for it directly. It comes as a by-product of the realization that everything is one, a by-product of comprehending that God exists in your enemy and in your friend.

The moment you become aware that you are not separate from existence, from all that is, that you are a part of it—and not a mechanical part but an organic part, just as a whale is organically joined to the ocean and is one with it all the time, just as my hand is organically one with me—then you can know love.

You can become aware of it only when you are non-ambitious. Only a non-ambitious mind is religious. It makes no difference what your ambition is . . . whether it is wealth, power or fame, or even liberation or God. If you are ambitious, that means your mind is moving somewhere else, running after something else. It is always busy achieving, it is never just being that which it already is.

Ambition is tension, and tension is the barrier to encountering the divine. Once you encounter it, you are no more—the encounter cleanses you completely, the encounter devours you completely. Only then is there love. The death of your ego is the birth of love.

Ordinarily, we think of love in contrast to hate. But those who know always think of love in contrast to *ego*. The real enemy of love is not hatred—the real enemy of love is ego. In fact, hatred and love as we know them are two aspects of the same coin.

Love comes when you are not, when the ego is not there. And the ego is not there, you are not, when you are not ambitious. A non-ambitious moment is a moment of meditation. In a non-ambitious moment, when you are seeking noth-

ing, asking for nothing, praying for nothing; when you are
totally satisfied with what you are, not comparing yourself
with anybody else—in that moment you touch the deep reservoir of the divine. You are not just in contact with it, you are
deeply in it: you are one with it.

Then love flows. Then you cannot do otherwise; you can
only be loving. Then love is not the opposite of hate; there is
neither love as we have known it nor hate as we have known
it; both have ceased. Now quite a different quality of love, in
a very new dimension, grows in you.

This love is a state of mind, not a relationship. It is not
related to anybody, it is not that you love someone, rather, it
is that you are *loving*. The other is not, the loved one is not,
you are just loving to whatsoever comes in contact with you.
You are love. You live *in love*. It has become your perfume.

Love is there, the perfume is there, even when you are
alone—like a flower on a lonely path. No one passes, but the
flower is there with its perfume. No one is there to know, to
enjoy, but the perfume goes on silently spreading because it is
not addressed to anyone. The perfume is there because that is
the manifestation of the innermost nature of the flower. The
flower is blissful, and the perfume is part of its nature. There
is no effort to spread it—it is effortless.

When ego is not, love comes as a perfume—as a flowering
of your heart. Then it goes on spreading. It is addressed to no
one, it is absolutely unaddressed. When love is not addressed,
it becomes prayer. When it is addressed, it degenerates into
sex; when it is unaddressed, it rises to prayer.

God or love or death are not problems to be solved—they
are experiences to be passed through. They are not questions
that can be answered; they are quests that can either be realized or not. God cannot be made a question at all. Whenever
you ask questions about God they are bound to be superficial.
And the answers are even more superficial, because a question
that is superficial can only be answered with an even more
superficial answer.

God is an existential quest; an inquiry, not a question. So

there is no ready-made answer to the question: Does God exist? Those who give ready-made answers to the question do not know anything at all. It cannot be said that God exists and it cannot be said that God does not exist. Both answers are irrelevant, because no answer can touch the real problem.

The theologies of every religion have become superficial because they have simply become expert in supplying ready-made answers: you ask, and the answer is supplied. But this has done a very subtle harm to the religious spirit. These things cannot be answered like that. You cannot ask someone, "What is love?" You cannot ask it! And if he answers, then he is in the same boat as you—neither of you knows.

We want answers because we are trying to escape from the suffering entailed in the process of love, in the process that is life, existence, God. We are riding safe vessels: we want to *know* so that we will not suffer. But suffering is birth; through suffering there is ecstasy. You have to pass through the dark night of the soul to come to the dawn. You cannot ask what dawn is. You have to pass through the dark night to know it.

God is a search, not a question, and a search cannot be answered. It has to be lived; you have to go into it deeply. You will have to be committed to it; you will have to throw yourself into it. That is what the fear is: throwing oneself into the unknown, the uncharted.

You are afraid, so you sit on the bank and ask questions. And, of course, there are always people who get pleasure out of answering you. To answer someone is ego-fulfilling: you know and the other does not, the other is ignorant and you are a knower. Then this mutual nonsense goes on: someone asks and someone will answer. Both are in ignorance because the problem cannot be solved on the bank. One has to go into unknown waters, and you cannot go into the unknown with ready-made answers.

Ready-made answers are a barrier to the unknown. One has to go into the unknown in total insecurity, not knowing anything. That is what is necessary—and nothing can be done about it. To jump into the unknown is to come upon the truth, the ecstasy. When you come upon the divine yourself, it is not simply an answer, it is a transformation: you become one with it.

You can never become one with any answer; an answer always remains separate in the memory. You can go on collecting answers and piling them up in the mind; then you know so many answers and yet the question remains the same—it is still not answered.

The question cannot be answered like that. It can only be answered through a mutation. When you encounter the divine directly, immediately—when the divine is before you and you are before the divine with no barrier in between—then you encounter the fire and you are transformed. Then you become one with the divine flame—you and the flame are not separate. Then you never ask, "What is God?" because you are not separate. Then you never answer the question "What is God?" because you are not separate.

Those who have known have remained silent. They have talked, but they have not given any answer to the question; they have made no statement at all. They have pointed in a certain direction, but to point is not to make a statement, it is just a gesture. Because of the limitation of words, of language—because of the limitations of the human mind, questioning and answering—one can only indicate, one can only point in a particular direction.

God is a living encounter, not a question. And through God, love comes. But one can only come to know God when one is not ambitious. Be non-ambitious and you will know.

Do not define yourself by those who are behind, because no one is behind, or with those who are ahead, because no one is ahead. Do not compare yourself with anybody. You are alone. Only you are like you. No one else is like you. Just be what you are.

That doesn't mean not to be active. Be active, but only because of yourself, not in comparison to others. Flower by yourself, not in comparison to others. With this attitude, when the mind is completely unmoving, something of the divine will lure you; you will have glimpses.

Once you know the bliss of such glimpses, you will know the nonsense, the absurdity, and the absolutely unnecessary misery of ambition. Then the mind stops by itself. It becomes completely still, silent, non-achieving. In this still moment, the jump comes. And after the jump, there is God. After the jump, there is love—love follows like a shadow.

NINE

The Unknown Life of Jesus

Was Jesus fully enlightened?

Yes, he was fully enlightened. But because he lived amidst a people who were absolutely ignorant about enlightenment, he had to speak in a language which may indicate he was not. He had to use such language because, at that particular time and place, there was no other possibility—only this could be understood. Languages differ. When a Buddha speaks he uses a language that is totally different. He cannot say, "I am the son of God" because to talk about "the son" or "the father" is just nonsense. But for a Jesus it is impossible to use any other language—Jesus is speaking to a very different type of person.

Yet in many ways, Jesus is connected to Buddha. Christianity has no knowledge of where Jesus was for thirty years. With the exception of two earlier incidents—when he was born, and once when he was seven years old—only the three years of his ministry are known; the remaining period is unknown. But India has many traditions about it: there are folk stories in Kashmir indicating that he was meditating in a Buddhist monastery there during all the years which are not accounted for.

Then, when he was thirty, he suddenly appeared in Jerusalem. Then he was crucified and there is the story of his resurrection. But again, where does he disappear to after he resurrects? Christianity has nothing to say about it. Where did he go? When did he die a natural death?

Miguel Serrano, in his book *The Serpent of Paradise*, writes: "Nobody knows what he did or where he lived until he was thirty, the year he began his preaching. There is a legend, however, that says he was in Kashir, the original name of Kashmir. *Ka* means 'the same as' or 'equal to' and *shir*, Syria."

It is also reported that a Russian traveller, Nicholas Nattovich, who came to India sometime in 1887, visited Ladakh in Tibet where he was taken ill and stayed in the famous Hemis Gumpa. During his stay in the Gumpa, he went through various volumes of Buddhist scriptures and literature wherein he found extensive mention of Jesus, his teaching, and his visit to Ladakh. Later Nattovich published the book, *Life of Saint Jesus*, in which he related all that he had found out about the visit of Jesus to Ladakh and to other countries in the East.

It is recorded that from Ladakh, after travelling through lofty mountain passes, along snowy paths and glaciers, Jesus reached Pahalgam in Kashmir. He lived there for a long period as a shepherd looking after his flock. It is here that Jesus found some traces of the lost tribes of Israel.

This village, it is recorded, was named Pahalgam, village of shepherds, after Jesus lived there. *Pahal* in Kashmiri means "shepherd" and *gam*, "a village." Later, on his way to Srinagar, Jesus rested and preached at Ishkuman/Ishmuqam, ("the place of rest of Jesus"), and this village was also named after him. When he was thirty, suddenly he appeared in Jerusalem and there follows the crucifixion and the story of the resurrection.

While Jesus was still on the cross, a soldier speared his body, and blood and water oozed out of it. The incident is recorded in the gospel of St. John: "But one of the soldiers with a spear pierced his side, and forthwith came there out blood and water." (John 19:34) This has led to the belief that Jesus was alive on the cross, because blood does not flow out of a dead body.

But Jesus must die. Either the crucifixion is complete and he dies or the whole of Christianity dies. Christianity depends on the miracle of the resurrection; it had been prophesied that the coming Christ would be crucified and then resurrected. Jesus was resurrected—it had to be so. If it were not so then the Jews would not believe that he was a prophet.

They waited for this, and it happened. After three days his body disappeared from the cave where it had been put and he was seen by at least eight people. Then Jesus disappeared again. Christianity has nothing to say about where he went after the resurrection and nothing has been recorded about when he died.

He came to Kashmir again and he lived there until he was 102, when he died. And the town, the exact place where this occurred, is known.

Did he live in Kashmir under another name?

No, not another name really. While those of you from the West call him Jesus, the whole Arabic world calls him Esus or Esau. In Kashmir he was known as Yousa-Asaf. His tomb is known as "the tomb of Yousa-Asaf who came from a very distant land and lived here." It is also indicated on the tomb that he came to live there 1900 years ago.

Miguel Serrano, the author of *The Serpent of Paradise*, who visited the tomb, writes:

"It was evening when I first arrived at the tomb, and in the light of the sunset the faces of the men and children in the street looked almost sacred. They looked like people of ancient times; possibly they were related to one of the lost tribes of Israel that are said to have immigrated to India. Taking off my shoes, I entered and found a very old tomb surrounded by a filigree stone fence which protected it, while to one side there was the shape of a footprint cut into the stone. It is said to be the footprint of Yousa-Asaf, and according to the legend, Yousa-Asaf is Jesus.

"On the wall of the building hangs an inscription and below it a translation from the Sharda into English which reads: YOUSA-ASAF (KHANYA, SRINAGAR)."

Jesus was a totally enlightened being. This phenomenon of resurrection seems inconceivable as far as Christian dogma is concerned, but not for yoga. Yoga believes—and there are ample proofs of it—that a person can totally die, without dying. The heart stops, the pulse stops, the breathing stops. Yoga even has methods that teach this. In India we know that Jesus must have practiced some deep yogic exercise when he was put on the cross because if the body really dies, there is no possibility of resurrection.

When those who had crucified Jesus felt that he was dead, his body was brought down from the cross and given to his followers. Then, after wrapping the body in thin muslin and an ointment, which even to this day is known as "the ointment of Jesus," two of his followers, Joseph and Nicodemus, removed the body to a cave, the mouth of which they blocked with a huge boulder.

There is one sect, the Essenes, that has its own tradition about it. It is said that Essene followers helped Jesus to recover from his wounds. When he was seen again, because his followers could not believe that he was the same Jesus who had been crucified, the only way—and this is recorded in the Bible—was to show them his healed wounds. Those wounds were healed by the Essenes, and the healing took place during the three days when Jesus remained in the cave recovering from his ordeal. Then, when the wounds were healed, he disappeared: the huge boulder at the mouth of the cave had been rolled away and the cave was found vacant. Jesus was not there! It is this disappearance of Jesus from the cave that has led to the common theory of his resurrection and ascent to heaven.

But after he had shown himself to his disciples he *had* to disappear from the country, because if he had remained there, he would have been crucified again. He went to India, into which, one tradition says, a tribe of the Jews had disappeared.

The famous French historian, Bernier, who visited India during the reign of Aurangzeb, wrote: "On entering the kingdom after crossing the Pir Panjal Pass, the inhabitants of the frontier villages struck me as resembling the Jews."

Yes, Kashmiris really do look Jewish—in their faces, in their every expression. Wherever you move in Kashmir, you feel that you are moving in a Jewish land. It is thought that Jesus came to Kashmir because it was a Jewish land in India— a tribe of Jews was living there. There are many stories in Kashmir about Jesus, but one has to go there to discover them.

The crucifixion changed Jesus' mind totally. From then on, he lived in India for seventy years continuously, in complete silence: unknown, hidden. He was not a prophet, he was not a minister, he was not a preacher. That is why not much is known about him.

Christianity lacks much. Even about Jesus it lacks much. His whole life is not known. What he practiced, how he meditated is not known. The Christian apostles who recorded what he said were ignorant people: they never knew much. One was a fisherman, another was a carpenter. All twelve apostles were ignorant.

The apostles didn't understand what Jesus was doing when he went to the hills and was silent for forty days. They only recorded that it happened and that when he came back again, he began preaching. But what was he doing there? Nothing is known, nothing.

After his period of silence, he became more and more involved in something which looked more social and political than religious. It had to be so, because the people around him were absolutely non-philosophical, so whatever he said was misunderstood. When he said, "I am the king of the Jews," he was not talking about a kingdom of this world; he was speaking in metaphors. Not only his enemies misunderstood him— even his followers and apostles misunderstood. They, too, began to think in terms of an earthly kingdom; they could not understand that what he was saying belonged to another world, that it was only symbolic. They also thought that Jesus was going to become king sooner or later.

That created the whole trouble. Jesus might not have been crucified in a different land, but for the Jews he was a problem. Jews are very materialistic. They were materialistic in the time of Jesus, and they still are. To them the other world is meaningless; they are only concerned with this world. Even if they talk of the other world, it is only as a prolongation of this world—not a transcendence but a continuity. They have a different way of thinking.

That is why, as far as the material sciences are concerned, the Jewish contribution is so great. It is not accidental. The person who is most responsible for molding the whole world in terms of a materialistic concept was a Jew, Karl Marx.

Karl Marx, Freud, Einstein—these three Jews are the builders of the twentieth century. Three Jews building the whole world! Why? No one exists in the world today who has not been influenced by the Jewish concept.

Jews are very down-to-earth, rooted in the earth, so when Christ began to talk like a Buddha, there was no meeting, no communion. He was continuously misunderstood.

Pilate was more understanding toward him than his own race. He continuously felt that an innocent man was being unnecessarily crucified and he tried his best not to crucify him. But then, there were political considerations.

Even when they were about to crucify Jesus, at the last moment, Pilate asked him a question: "What is truth?"

Jesus remained silent. It was a Buddhist answer. Only Buddha has remained silent about truth, no one else. Something has always been said—even if it is only that nothing can be said. Only Buddha has remained silent, totally silent. And Jesus remained silent. The Jews understood this to mean that he did not know. They thought, if he knows, then of course he will say. But I have always felt that Pilate understood. He was a Roman; he might have understood. But Pilate disappeared from the scene; he put the priests in total charge and just disappeared—he did not want to be involved.

This whole thing happened because there were two languages being used. Jesus was speaking of the other world—of course, in terms of this world—and the Jews took every word literally.

This would not have happened in India where there is a long tradition of parables, a long tradition of symbols. In India, the reverse misunderstanding is possible because the tradition has been going on for so long that someone speaking of this earth may be understood to be speaking of the other world. There are poets in India who talk about romance, love, and sex—of this world, totally of this world—but their followers interpret these as symbolic of the other world. Even if you talk about wine and women, they think that the wine means ecstasy and the women are *devas*. It happens!

Jews are literal, very literal. And incredibly, they have remained the same. They are a strange race, with a different outlook from the rest of the world. That is why they have never been at home anywhere. They cannot be, because they have a different type of mind. To penetrate a Jew is always difficult: he has a certain closedness, a certain defensiveness. And the longer Jews have been homeless, the more defensive they have become.

The basic thing about Jews is that they think in terms of matter—even God seems to be part of the material world. That is why it was impossible for them to understand Jesus. For example, Jews say that when someone does something wrong to you, you should do something wrong back to him— and with double the force. This is how matter behaves. React! If someone puts out one of your eyes, then put out both of his eyes.

Jesus began to say an absolutely contradictory thing: if someone slaps you on one side of the face then give him the other side also. This was absolutely Buddhist. One cannot really conceive of how a Jew could suddenly begin to talk like this. There was no tradition for it, no link with the past.

Nothing happens unless there is a cause. So Jesus is inconceivable as a Jew. He suddenly happens, but he has no roots in the past of Jewish history. He cannot be connected with it because he has nothing in common with it. As far as the Jewish God is concerned, Jesus' love, his compassion, is just nonsense.

You cannot conceive of a more jealous god, a more violent and angry god than the Jewish God. He could destroy a whole city in a single moment if someone disobeyed him. Then Jesus suddenly emerges and says, "God is love." It is inconceivable unless something else had penetrated the tradition.

When Buddha talks about compassion it is not inconceivable. The whole of India has been talking about it for centuries, and Buddha is part of the tradition. But Jesus is not part of the Jewish tradition. That is why he was killed, crucified.

No Buddha has ever been killed in India because, however rebellious, he still belongs to the tradition; however rebellious, he conforms to the deeper ideals. One even begins to think that he is more Indian than Indian society in general because he conforms more to the basic ideals of the country.

But Jesus was a total outsider in Jerusalem, using words and symbols, a language totally unknown to the Jews. He was bound to be crucified; it was natural. I see Jesus as living deep in meditation, deep in enlightenment, but involved with a race that was political—not religious, not philosophical.

Jews have not given great philosophers to the world. They have given great scientists but not great philosophers. The very mind of the race is different; it works in a different way. Jesus was just an outsider, a stranger. He began to create trouble; he had to be made silent.

Then he escaped and he never tried again. He lived in silence with a small group—working silently, esoterically. And I feel that there is still a hidden, esoteric tradition that continues. If one forgets Christianity and goes back to discover Jesus without the Christianity, one will be enriched. Christianity has become the barrier now.

Whenever you think about Jesus, the Christian interpretation of Jesus becomes the only interpretation. When the

Dead Sea Scrolls were found twenty years ago by the Dead Sea, they caused much agitation. The *Scrolls*, which were originally possessed by the Essenes, are more authentic than the Bible. But Christianity could not compromise. The *Dead Sea Scrolls* tell a different tale, a totally different story about the Jews. Even the Koran has a different story to tell. It seems that Mohammed also was in contact with many Jewish mystics.

This always happens. When I say something, I create two groups of people around me. One group will be exoteric: they will organize, they will do many things concerned with society, with the world that is without; they will help preserve whatsoever I am saying. The other group will be more concerned with the inner world. Sooner or later the two groups are bound to come in conflict with one another because their emphasis is different. The inner group, the esoteric mind, is concerned with something quite different from the exoteric group. And, ultimately, the outer group will win, because they can work as a group. The esoteric ones cannot work as a group; they go on working as individuals. When one individual is lost, something is lost forever.

This happens with every teacher. Ultimately the outer group becomes more and more influential; it becomes an establishment. The first thing an establishment has to do is to kill its own esoteric part, because the esoteric group is always a disturbance. Because of "heresy," Christianity has been destroying all that is esoteric.

And now the Pope is at the opposite extreme to Jesus: this is the ultimate schism between the exoteric and the esoteric. The Pope is more like the priests who crucified Jesus than like Jesus himself. If Jesus comes again, he will be crucified in Rome this time—by the Vatican. The Vatican is the exoteric, organizational part, the establishment.

These are intrinsic problems: they happen, and you cannot do anything about it.

Yes, Jesus *was* an enlightened being. Just like Buddha, Mahavir, Krishna.

In the Bible, many miracles are recorded. For example, the raising of Lazarus from the dead by Jesus after the body was already smelling. Is it possible for a dead man to be revived?

It is possible, but it is possible in a very different way—very different. If the person is really dead, if the body is dead, then it is not possible. But it may be that the person only *appears* to be dead . . .

But it states in the Bible that the body was already smelling.

The body may smell; the person may be in a deep coma and the body can begin to smell. There are other possibilities also, but the Jews of that time could not understand what those other possibilities were.

For example, your soul may be out of the body and yet connected to it. Then the body will be in a deep coma—and it has to be preserved or it will begin to deteriorate. It is a problem now: a very strong force is needed to bring the soul which is hovering around the body back to the body. But it can be revived, and a person like Jesus can help it to revive.

In India, we have many such events.

You may have heard the story about Shankara's great debate with Mandan Mishra, the great Indian scholar of dualism.

He came to debate with him, because that was the traditional way in India. It was not a fight but a very friendly discussion, and if one could convince the other, then the other would become his disciple. With this as the condition, the debate continued. Shankara would go from one village to another all over India in order to discuss the issue with Mandan Mishra. But there was a problem. Whom could they

138 • THE GREAT CHALLENGE

make the judge? They were both pillars: one of dualism and the other of non-dualism. Who would preside over the debate? No one was worthy of presiding. And who would be able to understand what they were saying? Who would know which one had been defeated and which one had won?

The only person possible was Mandan Mishra's wife, and it was rare to allow a woman to preside over such a debate. But there was no other alternative, so Mandan Mishra's wife was made the judge.

Finally, Mandan Mishra was defeated. But his wife declared that even though he was defeated, he was only half defeated because she was his other half. "So now, Shankara," she said, "you will have to debate with me!"

It was a trick! Now Shankara was in great difficulty. It was declared that Mandan Mishra was defeated but only by half because in India we say that a husband is only half a person, his wife is the other half, and it is the two halves which make one whole. So Mandan Mishra was only half defeated; half still remained.

"Now Mandan Mishra will preside and I will debate with you," said the wife. And she was really a rare woman—she began to discuss sex!

Shankara was at a disadvantage. He was a celibate, so now he felt that he was going to be defeated. He knew nothing about sex; the whole phenomenon was unknown to him. It was a trick and now he was caught; so he said, "First give me six months' leave so that I can learn about sex. Only then can I come and discuss it with you. Otherwise I am already defeated." And the six months' leave was granted.

Then there was another problem. The story is beautiful . . . Shankara had taken a vow of celibacy for the whole of his life and so he could not use his body for any experiments in sex. Therefore he had to leave his body and enter another body, leaving his own body with his disciples to be continuously guarded and preserved, because if anything happened to it, he would not be able to enter it again. For six months a group of twelve disciples kept a constant vigil: they remained with the body continuously.

A king had just died, so when Shankara entered the king's body, it was already dead. Then the dead body revived and Shankara lived inside the body for six months, deep in sexual experiments. The king's wife began to feel that something was different, but what could she do? The person was different but the body was the same. After six months, Shankara returned to his own body, the discussion took place, and Bharati, Mandan Mishra's wife, was defeated.

This is one possibility: Jesus may have helped to revive Lazarus who was not really dead but only appeared to be.

Christianity is unaware of many things. Lazarus may have been in a deep coma, and the body may have begun to deteriorate. And a coma can continue for years. I have seen one woman who was in a coma for nine months. If someone had not preserved the body, she would have died immediately. Everything had to be done for her. She was just lying there as if she were dead. She could not do anything for herself. Had she been forgotten for seven days she would have begun to smell, stink.

So Jesus might have helped a person who was in a coma, or a person whose soul, for whatever reason, was out of his body. A dead man cannot become alive again. If he comes alive it only means that he was not really dead. As far as I am concerned, no miracle happens in the world. Something appears to be a miracle because we do not know the whole story, we do not know the whole reason for it.

What about the other miracles reported in the Bible? For example, the one where Jesus fed thousands of people with two loaves of bread and five fish. Can you explain it?

Many things are possible. Nothing is a miracle, nothing. Even materialization is not a miracle; it is a science.

Materialization is possible. So are many other things.

Something can be brought here by an unknown route. You are not aware of the route, but something suddenly appears here. That is not materialization. A Swiss watch can be brought here from a store—spirits can help to bring it here. You will not see the spirits, only the watch. But that is not materialization. It is just a Swiss-made watch coming here via some route that is not known.

But materialization is also possible. Something coming out of nothing . . .

How is it possible?

When you ask how it is possible, that *how* is difficult to answer. You have to pass through a long, long practice to be able to do it.

Can you give an example of this?

The more capable your mind becomes of concentration, the closer you come to the point where materialization can happen. If you can be in absolute concentration, materialization can happen.

But with your mind the way it is, you cannot concentrate even for a single moment. If you can concentrate on something for a single moment, focusing your total mind for even one second—then you can will it to appear and it will appear.

But try it first in very easy ways. For example: you can take a glass, fill it with water, and then put some glycerin or oil on the surface of the water. Then float a very thin pin on the surface of oil or glycerin. Then concentrate on the pin. Concentrate! Without blinking, focus both your eyes on the pin for two minutes. After two minutes of concentration, begin to order the pin to go toward the right. Within seven days of practicing it, you will be able to move the pin.

Once a pin can follow orders from your mind, you have

achieved something that is needed for materialization. It is a long process, but now at least you can feel that mind does have power over matter. Once this power is felt, once you are *totally* able to concentrate, materialization becomes possible. Then only willing is needed, nothing else. If the mind is totally concentrated on making a rose appear, then a rose will appear.

Because of this, Indians have always said that the whole world is just a dream in the mind of the divine. God dreams something, and it appears. When he stops dreaming, it dissolves.

Are you yourself able to make things materialize?

I am able to do it. And I am also able *not* to do it—because I feel the absurdity of it. And the second ability is better. Buddha could not be persuaded to do it, but Jesus *had* to do it. Again, the reason is the same: because the Jews could not believe anything unless it was something material. They could not be convinced without a miracle.

In India one can conceive of a Buddha who does not perform any miracles. But the Jews began to ask, "Can you do miracles? Only if you do miracles can we believe that what you are saying is meaningful." It was not Jesus who wanted to do the miracles, it was the Jews who compelled him. Without miracles, his thinking, his preaching, would have seemed meaningless to them.

We cannot even conceive of Buddha's doing miracles. It is appealing to a much lower state of mind. Why be so concerned with convincing anyone? Why be so concerned? Sometimes a miracle would happen around Buddha, but it was not deliberately done. It would happen in a particular situation.

Still, there are layers of meaning to it. All the miracles recorded in the Bible—sometimes bread appears, sometimes disease disappears, or a dead man becomes alive again—are all very material, very ordinary things. They are concerned with the day-to-day problems of the ordinary man: bread, disease, death.

Buddha says that the whole of life is a dream. So what does it matter if someone becomes alive again? It is meaningless. It only means that a particular dream has begun to have some reality again.

There is one story recorded. Buddha was in a certain village where a child had died. The mother was so obsessed with the child that she was weeping and crying and trying to escape in order to commit suicide. So someone said, "Come to see Buddha. He can do anything. He is an enlightened man; anything is possible. Come! He is the compassionate one. If he begins to feel compassionate toward you, the child may revive."

So she came to Buddha with the dead child in her arms and laid the child at Buddha's feet. Imagine what would have happened to Jesus in a similar situation in a Jewish country. If the child had not been brought back to life, Jesus would have been finished completely because this would have *proven* that he was not the man he claimed to be.

But when the child was brought to Buddha, what did he say? He said to the mother, "I will make your child alive again, but first you will have to do one thing. Go to every house in the city and find out if there is any house where no one has ever died. If there is any house in the village where no one has ever died, then in the evening I will revive your child."

The woman went and asked everyone. In every house, in every family, someone had died. By the time she returned in the evening she had become aware that death is a reality, death is a part of life.

Buddha asked her, "What do you say now? Is there any house, any family, any person who has not suffered due to someone's death?"

The woman said, "I have not returned now so that my

child can be revived. I have come to be initiated. Death is a reality. The child has gone, I will go, everyone will have to go. Initiate me into that life which never ends."

This is a greater miracle! But we cannot conceive of it. If the child had been brought back to life, it would have been a miracle. But this is a greater miracle, with deeper compassion. With a particular race it is possible. Otherwise, it is not possible. The woman became a sannyasin: the death of the child was not used to satisfy the lust for life, it was used for renunciation.

If Buddha's disciples were hungry, he would not perform a miracle and provide them with bread. On the contrary, he would say, "Witness your hunger. Witness the hunger so that you can transcend it, so that you can move away from it. The hunger is not you; it is somewhere on the periphery. Remember that. Use it." Jesus had to supply bread and Buddha had to convince his followers to fast. To give someone bread is not a miracle really, but to make someone ready to fast *is* a miracle.

It depends on how we define things. I am not concerned with miracles because it is all nonsense. This whole life that we are living is absurd, so even if you can create something in it, it is meaningless. The only miracle that I am interested in is pushing you beyond. Even a glimpse of the beyond will be a miracle.

As I see it, if Jesus had prevented himself from doing these things, he would have served humanity better—by doing them, he attracted fools. The masses became interested in Jesus only because of his so-called miracles. He tried to help them through his miracles but it was not possible; on the contrary, he himself got into trouble. I do not see that Christ was able to help anyone in this way.

If I were to materialize something, it would be bound to happen that fools would gather round me more and more. Soon I would be amongst fools, because only they are interested in such things.

If you go to Sai Baba you will see that he is doing certain things. But then only fools are attracted. If a ring appears in my hand, what does it matter? How is it related to any spiritual phenomenon? Even if this whole house disappears and then reappears again, what does it matter? So what? That is why I am not concerned with miracles. And those who are only attract fools.

In comparing Jesus to Buddha, Jesus seems very active and revolutionary. Why is this?

There is a reason. But first, some explanation is needed.

Yoga divides man into two parts: the sun part and the moon part. The sun is symbolic of inner positivity and the moon is symbolic of inner negativity. "Sun" does not mean the outer sun nor does "moon" mean the outer moon. These words are used for the inner universe.

There is even one breath that is known as the sun breath and another breath that is known as the moon breath. Every forty to sixty minutes, your breath changes from one nostril to the other. If you need more heat in the body, or if you suddenly grow angry, your sun breath starts functioning. Yoga says that if you use your moon breath when you are angry, then you cannot be angry at all, because the moon breath creates a deep coolness inside.

The negative is cool, silent, still. The positive is hot, vibrant with energy, active. The sun is the active part in you and the moon is the inactive part in you. When one first becomes acquainted with the sun, the light is burning hot, like a flame.

If you analyze the inner life of Buddha or of Jesus with this distinction in mind, many things which are ordinarily hidden will become apparent. For example, whenever an enlightened one like Buddha is born, his early life will be very revolutionary. The moment one enters the inner dimension, the first experience is of a fiery flame. But the older Buddha grows, the more an inner coolness is felt. The more perfect the moon stage becomes, the more the revolutionary fervor is lost. That is why Buddha's words are not revolutionary.

Jesus did not have this opportunity. He was crucified while he was still a revolutionary and he died, as far as Christianity is concerned, at the age of thirty-three. If you compare Buddha's sayings with those of Jesus there is a clear-cut difference. Jesus' sayings look like those of a young man—hot. Buddha's early sayings were also like this, but he was not crucified for them; he lived to be eighty.

The reason he was not crucified is that India has always known that this happens. Whenever a person moves within, whenever a Buddha enters into himself, his first expression is fiery, revolutionary, rebellious. He bursts open and explodes into fire. But then that phase disappears and ultimately there is only the moon: silent, without any fire, with only light. That is why India has never killed anyone; that is why India has never behaved the way the Greeks behaved with Socrates or the Jews with Jesus.

Jesus was crucified early. Christianity still remains incomplete because Christianity is based on the early Jesus, on Jesus when he was just a flame. Buddhism is complete. It has known Buddha in all his stages. It has known Buddha's moon in all the stages of the moon—from the first day to the full-moon light.

It has been a misfortune for the West, it has proven itself to be one of the greatest misfortunes in history, that Jesus was crucified when he was just a flame, when he was only thirty-three. The flame would have turned into moonlight, but the opportunity was not given. The reason is that the Jews were not aware of the inner phenomenon.

India has known many Buddhas, and it is always true that whenever someone enters the inner dimension, he has to feel the fire of the revolutionary side coming up. If one continues going inward, this dissolves, and then there is only silence, a moonlit silence.

To change heat into light is the secret science of inner

alchemy. To change coal into diamonds, to change baser metals into gold—these are just symbols. Alchemists were never really concerned with changing baser metals into higher metals, but they had to hide what they were doing: they had to create an esoteric, secret symbology, because it was very difficult in early times to talk about an inner science and not be murdered. Jesus was killed: he was an alchemist. And the Christianity that developed after Jesus went against him. The Christian Church began to kill and murder those who were practicing the alchemy of inner transformation.

Christianity could not really flower into a religion; it remained a clerical thing. It could not create sannyasins, it could only create preachers—trained, dead, disciplined.

If Jesus was still in a rebellious and active stage at the time of the crucifixion, does that mean that he had not achieved the total spiritual growth and inner silence of Buddha?

At the time of the crucifixion he had just entered the moon center. But only on that very day! That has to be understood.

The Jesus of the Bible is not like Buddha, Mahavir, or Lao Tzu. You cannot conceive of Buddha's going into a temple and beating money lenders. But Jesus did it.

There were many different activities connected with the great temple of Jerusalem—there was a great money-lending business which exploited the whole country. People would come for an annual gathering and for other gatherings during the year, and obtain money at the temple at a high rate of interest. Then it would be impossible to repay and they would lose everything. The temple was becoming richer and richer: it was religious imperialism. The whole country was poor and suffering, but so much money would be automatically coming into the temple. Then Jesus entered one day with a whip in his hand. He overturned the money lenders' boards and began to beat the money lenders. He created chaos in the temple.

You cannot conceive of Buddha's doing this. Impossible! Jesus was the first communist: he was fiery, rebellious. That is why Christianity could give birth to communism. Hinduism could not give birth to it, no other religion could give birth to it; it is impossible. Only Christianity could do it, because with Jesus it has a relevance. The very language he used was totally different. He got so angry at some things that we cannot even believe it: he cursed a fig tree which was not yielding any fruit because he and his disciples were hungry. He destroyed it!

He threatened in a type of language that Buddha could not even utter. For example, he said that those who would not believe in him and the kingdom of God would be thrown into the fires of hell, the eternal fires of hell, and they would not be able to come back. Only the Christian hell is eternal. Every other hell is just a temporary punishment: you go there, you suffer, you come back. But Jesus' hell is eternal.

This looks unjust, absolutely unjust. Whatsoever the sin, eternal punishment cannot be justified. It cannot be! And what are the sins? Bertrand Russell has written a book, *Why I Am Not a Christian*, and one of the reasons he gives is that Jesus seems absurd. Russell says, "If I confess all the sins that I have committed, and all those sins which I have just thought about but never committed, you cannot give me more than five years' imprisonment. But eternal hell?"

Jesus speaks the language of a revolutionary when he talks about eternal, non-ending punishment—revolutionaries always look to the opposite end, to the extreme. You cannot conceive of Buddha's saying it or Mahavir's saying it, but Jesus says that a camel can pass through the eye of a needle sooner than a rich man can enter the kingdom of God. He cannot pass! This is the seed of communism, the basic seed.

Jesus was a revolutionary. He was not only concerned with spirituality but with economics, politics—everything. Had he been only a spiritual man he would not have been crucified, but because he became a danger to the whole social structure, to the status quo, he was crucified.

He was not a revolutionary like Lenin or Mao but still, Mao and Lenin and Marx are inconceivable without there having been a Jesus in history. They belong to the same path as Jesus: the early Jesus, the fiery man—rebellious, ready to destroy everything—the Jesus who was crucified.

But Jesus was not simply a revolutionary; he was also a spiritual man. He was, somehow, a mixture of Mahavir and Mao. The Mao was crucified and only the Mahavir remained in the end. The day Jesus was crucified was not only the day of his crucifixion, it was the day of his inner transformation also.

When Jesus remained silent after Pilate asked him, "What is truth?" he was behaving like a Zen Master. If you look at the previous life of Jesus, if you look at his whole previous life, this silence was not like Jesus at all. What happened? Why did he not speak? Why was he at a loss? He was one of the greatest orators the world has ever produced; we may even say, without hesitation, the greatest. His words were so penetrating. He was a man of words, not a man of silence. Why did he suddenly remain silent?

He was moving toward the cross. Pilate asked him, "What is truth?" Jesus had spent his whole life talking about truth; he was defining only that, that is why Pilate asked him. But he remained silent.

What happened in Jesus' inner world has never been reported because it is difficult to report. Christianity has allowed it to remain submerged because what happened in the inner world of Jesus can only be interpreted in India, nowhere else. Only India knows about the inner changes, the inner transformation that happens.

What happened was this: Jesus is suddenly on the verge of crucifixion. He is about to be crucified and now his whole revolution is meaningless. Everything that he has been saying is futile, everything that he has been living for is coming to an end. Everything is finished. And because death is so near, he must now move within. No time can be lost, not a single moment can be lost. He must come to the end of his journey now, and before he is crucified he must complete the inner journey.

All along he had been on an inner journey. But because he was also entangled with outer problems he could not move to that cool point, the moon point; he remained fiery, hot. But it may be that he did this consciously.

Jesus was a disciple of John the Baptist who was a great revolutionary and spiritual leader. John the Baptist had waited for Jesus for many years. Then, on the day he initiated Jesus in the River Jordan, he said to Jesus, "Now take over my work and I will disappear. It is enough." And from that day on, he was rarely seen again; he disappeared. In the words of the inner language, he disappeared from the sun point and moved to the moon point; he became silent. He had done his work and had now given the work to someone who would complete it.

On the day of the crucifixion, Jesus must have become aware that now his work was finished. "There is no longer any possibility of doing anything more now. I must move within. The opportunity must not be lost." That is why, when Pilate asked him what truth is, he remained silent. Because of this, the miracle happened which has remained an enigma for Christianity. Because of *this*.

As he was moving to his cooler side, to the moon center, he was crucified. When someone comes to the moon center for the first time, his breathing stops. Because breathing, too, is an activity of the sun point. Now everything becomes silent, everything is as if dead. They thought he was dead, but he was not: he had simply come to the moon center where breathing stops. No outgoing breath, no ingoing breath—the gap.

When one remains in the gap, there is such a deep balance that it is a virtual death. But it is *not death*. The crucifiers, the murderers of Jesus, thought that he was dead so they allowed his disciples to bring the body down. But he was not dead, and when the cave was opened after three days he was not there. The "dead" body had disappeared. After three days, Jesus was seen again by four or five people. But no one would believe them when they went to the villages to say that Jesus was resurrected. No one would believe it.

When he escaped from Jerusalem, Jesus went to Kashmir, where he remained. But then his life was not the life of Jesus but the life of Christ. Jesus was the sun point and Christ the moon point. From then on, he remained totally silent. That is why there is no record of him. He would not talk, he would not deliver any message, he would not preach. He remained in Kashmir, not as a revolutionary but as a Master—living in his own silence. A few people travelled to be with him. Those who became aware of his presence in Kashmir without having had any outward information about it would travel to him. And really, there were not so few—maybe only a few in comparison to the world—but there were many.

Christianity is incomplete because it knows only the early, revolutionary Jesus. And because of that, Christianity could give birth to communism. But Jesus himself died as a fully enlightened man—a full moon.

TEN

Out of Nothing . . .

*Were all souls created together, as Paul
Brunton theorizes, or were they created at
separate stages? Is this difference—the
difference in their stages—due to their own
choice or is it their destiny? What degree
of choice do we have as far as reincarnation
is concerned?*

Before I can answer this question, two or three things
must be understood. One, religious inquiry is basically different from scientific inquiry. In scientific inquiry the question is
important, but in religious inquiry it is the questioner—the
state of mind in which the question is asked—who is significant. In scientific questioning your mind has to be continuously focused on the question. In religious inquiry the
question is just a jumping board into something that is uncharted. So ask the question and then forget it, because the
question is concerned with the known and the answer can
only be concerned with the unknown.

When we formulate a question the very formulation, and
the presupposition on which the formulation is based, belong
to our mind, our memory, our knowledge. But the answer is
bound to be in a totally different dimension. For example,
this question. We will take it in parts.

Were all souls created together, as Paul Brunton theorizes, or are they created at separate stages?

The question seems relevant. Man has always been deeply concerned with the concept of creation: How are things created? When? Why? By whom? Even concerning souls man has many questions: When were souls created? Were they created equal or unequal? And if they were created equal, then why this inequality?

Is this difference—the difference in their stages—due to their own choice, or is it their destiny?

To us it seems important to ask about creation. But in existence, nothing is created; it is a continuous and endless beginning. The very concept of creation is childish and irrelevant as far as existence is concerned. The existence has always been: it has never been created and it can never be destroyed. "Creation" means "out of nothing"—and out of nothing, nothing can come. The world, the creation, is in constant change, but nothing can be created or destroyed.

Change is the reality. By "change" I mean that only the form changes, never the substance. The basic remains always the same; only the mode of expression, the form, changes. And this change is continuous; it is eternal.

So neither things nor souls are created. When not even things are created, the concept of the creation of souls becomes absurd. A created soul cannot be a soul; if a soul could be created then it would become just a thing.

But to the so-called religious mind creation seems significant, because we have conceived of God as the creator, and without creation where will the creator be? God is not the creator; God is existence itself. God is not something separate but the very substance of reality; he is not the creator of reality but the reality itself.

This duality—God and the world, the creator and the created—is due to our dualistic thinking. Our mind goes on creating dualities. But the reality is one; God is not the creator but the creation: the energy, the force, the basic substance of all.

Look at it in another way. No one asks, "Who created God?" because the question seems absurd. If you ask, "Who created God?" the question leads to an infinite regression: the same question can be asked again and again about the answer. If A created B then we can ask who created A. We can go on asking *ad infinitum* and no answer will be found. Every answer will only create another question—and the same question at that.

We cannot think of God as being created because if he is created then he is not God; he becomes a thing. The same is true of the soul: the soul is not a created phenomenon. And not only the soul—even matter is not a created phenomenon.

Even science realizes now that nothing can be created and nothing can be destroyed. Even if matter is converted into energy and energy converted into matter, it is not destruction and it is not creation. The quantity remains the same. If matter is converted into energy we can say that it is destroyed, because the matter disappears. But it is not destroyed, because matter itself is a form of energy—it is in a different form now, but the same energy remains.

The total quantity of existence is always the same. Whether you change A to B or B to C makes no difference to the total; not a single particle can be added to the total and not a single particle can be subtracted. And this total quantity is God.

The first thing to be understood is that nothing has been created. Existence *is*. Existence exists with no beginning and no end, but with many changes.

Our mind has created a second duality: that of matter and mind, body and soul. This, again, is a mind-created difference;

in reality, only one exists. "Body" is a form of it and "soul" is also a form of it.

That is why, just as matter can be converted into energy and energy can be converted into matter, the body is constantly being converted into consciousness and consciousness is constantly being converted into the body. You cannot come to a point where you can say the body ends and consciousness begins; there is no demarcation. Body and soul are not two things but only two poles of one existence: at one pole you feel the body and at the other there is consciousness.

You have an existence: one pole of it is consciousness; the other, the body. If you become more and more conscious, you become a soul; if you become less and less conscious, you become only a body. If Buddha is sitting beside you, both of you have bodies—but only to outward appearances. Buddha has no body; he is just a soul. By "soul" I mean that every particle of his existence has become aware. On the other hand, when you are in deep sleep, you are just a body and not a soul. You have no soul—just a concept of the soul, just a thought, a theory, a philosophy of the soul.

It may seem strange, but Gurdjieff used to say that not everyone has a soul. He also used to say that to have a soul is an achievement; only rarely does it happen that someone acquires a soul. He was right. The concept that everyone has a soul is misleading. It appears as if the soul is something you already have, but it is not so. It is a possibility, a potential: it is a flowering.

You *can* be a soul, but you may also miss. If your whole consciousness becomes an actuality, if the potential becomes an actual center of perfect awareness, then the attachment to the body will be lost. You will appear to be a body to others, but for you there will be no body.

This duality must be thrown away. "Body" means unconscious energy and "soul" means conscious energy. The energy is the same. Look at it in this way: "matter" means only one thing, potential soul, and "soul" means only matter that has come to its flowering. Forget completely the concept of creation and forget any concept of duality. Only then can you go deep into existence as it is.

Philosophies and theologies will not help—they are all mental creations. Whatsoever mind can create will be in the shape of duality. Wherever there is mind, there is bound to be duality, because mind cannot conceive of polar opposites as one.

How can mind conceive of body and soul as one? It is impossible. That is why there are two types of monists. One type is like Marx, Engels, Lenin, and Mao. They are monists: they say that there is no soul, that only matter and body exist. Mind cannot conceive of these two opposites existing side by side. Where will they meet, and how? The mind always inquires how consciousness and matter can meet—what the bridge between the two will be, and who will bridge them.

The question exists for the mind because the mind has already divided them. Then the question arises how they are able to work together along parallel lines. But they are *already bridged.* For example, if your body feels hurt, the mind is hurt. If there is a thorn in the body, you feel it in your soul. Your mind is depressed and your body becomes depressed; your mind feels blissful and the whole body becomes young and fresh. They do not behave as two, they behave as one.

But the mind divides them so there is a problem: how to make them behave as one, how to bridge the gap? Consciousness and matter are so opposite—what type of interrelationship can exist between them?

A monist will do one of two things. He may deny the soul completely, as materialists such as Marx, Engels, Lenin, and Mao have always done. Then only the body exists, there is no soul—the soul is just a fiction. Or there is another type of monist, like Shankara, who has said that there is no body, only the soul. Their conclusions are contradictory, but their logic, their argument, their thinking, is the same. Shankara says that matter is just an illusion, a dream—it cannot exist—and Marx says that the soul is just an illusion. The problem for both Shankara and Marx is this: first they make a division of body

156 • THE GREAT CHALLENGE

and soul and then they cannot unite them. It becomes a problem to unite them, so instead, they eliminate one or the
other.

To me, the solution to the whole problem takes on a different shape. Do not divide them. They are not two, they are
already one—they have *always* been one. When the energy
becomes conscious it is soul, when it becomes unconscious it
becomes body. Sometimes you are more a soul and less a
body, sometimes you are more a body and less a soul. This
flickering back and forth between one and the other goes on
continuously. In the morning you may be more a soul, in the
evening you are more a body. When you are in anger you are
more a body, when you are in love you are more a soul. The
degrees change continuously. When you meditate your consciousness expands and your body shrinks; when you take an
intoxicant your consciousness shrinks and your body expands.
Body and consciousness are two poles of one phenomenon.

So remember: this second duality is only mind-created,
mind-conceived. It is not there.

I will not say that souls were created. *Nothing* has been
created; everything has always been here. And when I say that
souls are not created, then of course, there is no question of
whether they were created equal or unequal. The question
will take on an altogether different shape.

As I see it, all souls are potentially equal. They have always been potentially equal, but in actuality they are not
equal. And *they* are responsible for it, no one else. No one
else is there to be responsible for it.

"God" is a very useful concept—you can put all your re-
sponsibilities on him. It is a good device, a very cunning device: if there is a God, and if you are not equal, then he is
responsible for it. He created you unequal so what can you
do? There is no such "God"! The total existence is God. You
participate in the total, so you participate in the responsibility.

You are potentially equal. That means you become equal

when you flower totally. A Buddha flowering, a Mahavir, a Jesus, a Mohammed—they become equal. There is no difference between them. But when the flowering was just a potential, they were unequal. On the path we are all unequal.

No one else is responsible because there *is* no one else. Only you exist. So it is your decision what to be or what not to be. Whatever you are is your decision. If you are not changing, it is your decision. If you want to change you can change this very moment. Time is not needed, only your decision to change.

If your decision is weak, more time is needed. But if your decision is total, then the change can happen this very moment. No time is needed—the change can occur this very moment! Time is needed only because your will is not total, your decision is not total. The problem is created because basically you are not ready to change, and yet your mind has become obsessed with the concept of change.

We have seen Buddha, so the greed is with us: how to be a Buddha? This is greed, this is lust, this is desire: how to be a Buddha—calm and collected, a light unto oneself, a deep silence with no disturbance, a flower not of this world. The greed has commenced, but the mind is not ready. We want to be like Buddha without being Buddha-like, because the mind wants other things also. What Buddha renounces we are not ready to renounce, but what Buddha has achieved we are greedy to achieve. This is the problem. The major part of your mind is not ready for the change, not ready to be a soul, but the desire has come in.

No one else is responsible for this. Go inside and analyze why you are not a Buddha. The potential is there, the energy is there. Why are you not a Buddha? Don't go on thinking: who created us unequal? Who created someone a Buddha and someone not a Buddha?

No one has created this; our minds are responsible. If I cling to the theory that God created us—him like a Buddha and me not like a Buddha—then what can I do? It is a destiny that has been forced on me. Then I can remain what I am, I can drift. This drifting will not do! The theory is just a saving device, a trick, so that you can continue as you are without bothering to change.

Religiousness is born in you only when you begin to feel total responsibility for yourself. Philosophy is one thing: philosophy can continue its meaningless, absurd theorizing. Religion is different: religion is a decision, it is to feel totally responsible for yourself. Whatever I am—a violent, angry, greedy, lust-filled mind, a bundle of desires—I am responsible.

The moment I feel that my ugliness is my responsibility, that my sin-centered mind is my responsibility, then the jump becomes possible. Because I am responsible for my ugliness, no one else can be responsible for my beauty. If I am responsible for all the darkness that is within me, then all the light that comes to a Buddha can also come to me. By taking responsibility for the one, the other potential becomes open.

Responsibility means freedom, so don't go on complaining to God. There is no one to receive your complaints; you are only deceiving yourself. If I am not responsible for myself then I am not free. But if I am free, then I have to carry the whole responsibility. If I am living in hell, it is my decision. I have used my energy and freedom in order to come to this hell; I have not been thrown there. Sartre speaks about man's being "thrown" into the world. No one has thrown you; it has been your choice to come.

Sartre feels that only in one dimension does man seem to be free, and that is suicide. You are not responsible for your birth, but you can be responsible for your death: you can commit suicide. This is illogical! If one pole is free, the opposite pole cannot be otherwise. If I can commit suicide—if I can end my life by my own decision—then, whether I remember it or not, my entry into life has also been my decision. The other pole must be consistent. If I am responsible for my suffering then no one else can be responsible for my bliss. If I can be responsible for my death then I am also responsible for my birth.

That is what religion says: that it is your freedom to be

born, to live, or to die. When someone is dying, to us he appears to be dying. But if you penetrate a dying man's mind you will see that he is desiring life and more life; he is constantly thinking of another life, of continuity. First he will try to cling to this life; then, if the clinging becomes impossible, he will desire a different body, a different form, a different shape, so that he can live again. But if a man is dying with no desires left unfulfilled, with no desire to continue living, then there will be no more births for him. If some desire is left unfulfilled, the mind will endeavor to fulfill it: that will become the choice for a new birth.

We know that when someone is born he has to die, but we do not know the other side of it: that when someone dies he has to be born again. If birth leads to death, then death will lead to birth again *unless you die totally.* That total death is *samadhi.* That total death is the highest peak of being a soul—the soul has been purified completely. There is no more desire for the future, because future means birth; no more desire for tomorrow, because tomorrow means birth; no more desire for the next moment, because the next moment means birth. In this moment, if you can die totally—with no future, with no tomorrow, with no desire, with nothing remaining unfulfilled—then there is no more birth.

It is your choice to be born again even though it is a very unconscious choice. If you become more conscious you will not choose, or you will choose differently.

Buddha was dying. Someone asked him, "Where will you be after death?"

Buddha said, "Nowhere. Enough! I have been in so many bodies for so many lives. It is enough. This time I am going to be nowhere. I am dying totally."

To the questioner this seemed tragic—Buddha, dying totally. He would not be born again. Now there was no hope left. The questioner began to weep.

Buddha said, "Don't weep. Dance! This is the moment of my fulfillment. I am dying totally. This is the last peak, the highest possibility. With no desire, with no hope, with no future, I am simply dissolving into the cosmos. I will be nowhere because I will be everywhere. You will not be able to find me confined to any point, but I will be like the salt of the earth: you will be able to taste me everywhere. But it will only be a taste. I will have no body, no visible form; I will be cosmic energy."

This is what Buddha means by *nirvana*. *Nirvana* is a beautiful word. It is not *moksha*, not liberation; *nirvana* is a different word, with a different quality. It means cessation—like the cessation of a candle. "Just like a candle ceases," Buddha says, "I will cease." When a candle ceases can you tell where the light has gone? You will not be able to find the flame, you will not be able to locate it, because now there is no new desire. But it will still be part of the cosmos, because nothing can disappear from the cosmos.

Everything is a choice. For us, this becomes difficult to conceive of, because then our whole suffering is our own choice. That is the problem. If someone else is responsible I can be at ease; then I am not suffering because of myself. If there is a destiny, if there is a God, then someone else is responsible and I am forced to be as I am. This is an escape. No one is there! You are alone.

Then how can we explain suffering? We think that we never choose suffering, but that is nonsense—we choose everything. No one is ready to admit that he chooses suffering because when we choose, we only choose façades. But in the end the reality of what we have chosen is encountered.

Everyone chooses pleasure and, ultimately, everyone suffers, because pleasure is just a façade, a false screen. The closer you come to pleasure, the more the pleasure begins to evaporate. This happens every time, but we are still not aware that pleasure is just the false face of pain, of suffering, of anguish.

No one chooses suffering directly; everyone chooses it indirectly. But the choice is unconscious, unaware. You choose

pleasure, and you have chosen suffering: every pleasure ends
in pain, every pleasure creates a tense state of mind. Suffering
is an inevitable part of pleasure, the tail end. You cannot
escape it. The hankering for pleasure, the seeking of pleasure,
is an illusion; what you achieve finally is never pleasure.

Look at it from the outside. Someone chooses pleasure. It
is a positive effort: ambition, achievement. Then suffering
comes—you choose heaven and you enter hell. Heaven is the
gate of hell. Enter the gate, and you have entered hell. Pleasure is a positively sought thing; happiness is negative. It is
not the presence of anything, it is the absence of something—
the absence of suffering. Don't choose pleasure, and suffering
will be discarded automatically. And when there is neither
pleasure nor suffering, there is happiness and bliss. From the
outside it looks negative—it is an absence—but from the inside
it is a positive thing. Happiness is your nature. It is also a
choice—everything is your choice. If you don't choose pleasure then you have chosen happiness.

Any moment you can change. And when I say "any moment" I mean much by it. I mean that whatever you have
chosen in the past is not a barrier. For millennia you may
have continuously chosen pleasure, pleasure, pleasure, and
perhaps got only suffering, suffering, suffering. But that is not
a barrier. Whatever you have chosen in the past you have
suffered for—nothing remains suspended in the balance. This
very moment you can choose the opposite and whatever *kar-
mas*, whatever actions you have done in the past, will not be a
barrier.

The mind can play tricks. If there is no destiny, if there
is no God, then *karma* becomes your scapegoat. You say,
"What can I do? I have been a sinner for lives and lives, and
now my *karma* is standing in the way. How can I choose
freely? I am bound by my *karma.*"

You are not in any bondage. And if you are, if you still
feel that there is an imprisonment around you, it is your own
choice. There is no prison and no jailor. You can come out
this very moment. It is your choice to live in a prison, it is

your choice to be there or not be there; no one is preventing you from leaving it.

If you want to be a prisoner you can create a philosophy around yourself in which you can be a prisoner. If you want to be a free man, if you want to be freedom itself, then you can choose a different type of thinking and you can be free. Both are your choices. Whatever level you are on *you* are responsible for because you are free; there is no bondage. There are many bondages, but there are no bondages outside you. They are all your creations: they are all because of you.

If you find difficulty in leaving the prison it is not the prison which is preventing you, it is your own habit, your own wrong choice. You have chosen it so many times that it has become a routine, a habit: it is easier to be in the prison than to be out of it.

You have become so well acquainted with the prison, you have decorated it so much that it looks not like a prison but like a home. Inside there is every security, every defense, and outside you will be vulnerable and open—with no defense, with no security. You will be in an unknown world, fear will grip you. It is new; it is not the prison of your own mind.

Whenever someone chooses, becomes conscious and remembers his freedom, he is free. It is this *remembrance* that makes him free. It is not an effort, it is coming to understand one's freedom and one's responsibility. Freedom and responsibility are two aspects of one coin, so don't throw your responsibility on anyone else or you will be throwing away your freedom also.

Feel responsible, accept responsibility for yourself, because only then will you become free. If you can say that this hell you are in is your choice, that no one else is responsible for it, then you have become free; you can go out of it, you can leave it. But if someone else has put you in this hell then only he can take you out. You are not involved in it at all.

The attitude that someone else has been the source of whatever you are will make you more of a body and less of a soul. I am saying that if you feel responsible for yourself, then a sudden freedom begins to appear in you. *You* are responsible for yourself; you become more of a soul.

A person like Buddha feels responsible for the whole world: Buddha goes to the other extreme. He says, "Whenever I choose misery I create vibrations of misery." A miserable person creates a certain type of vibration. A violent person creates violence, an angry person creates anger, a loving person creates love.

Ordinarily, we feel that God is responsible for us, the whole is responsible for us. Buddha goes to the other extreme and says, "I am responsible for the whole. If there is ugliness in the world I am responsible for it because I have created it. If there is hatred in the world I am responsible for it because I have created it. I have chosen hatred so many times when I could have chosen love. I have chosen hatred, I have chosen anger, I have chosen lust, and when I choose, I create a milieu in which others become vulnerable to choosing the same things."

If you feel that you are responsible for yourself then you become a soul. If you feel that you are responsible for the whole then you become a god. Then there are no barriers: you have become the whole—the "other" has gone.

What degree of choice do we have as far as reincarnation is concerned?

You are *totally* free to choose. Freedom cannot have degrees. How can freedom have degrees? How can you call that which has degrees "freedom?" If you are free only inside your house but not if you go outside, then you are not free. A limited freedom is not freedom; it is slavery with a beautiful name. Freedom means that which is unlimited. It cannot mean anything else. Slavery means limitation. This is something that has to be understood deeply. Slavery can never be unlimited—you cannot make someone a slave without limitations—because slavery is a limited thing. There *are* degrees of slavery: you can be more of a slave or less of a slave. I can make you a slave up to a certain limit; I can say, "As far as this or that is concerned, you are free." But there are no degrees of freedom; freedom is total. It is such an infinite phenomenon that we become afraid of it.

Erich Fromm has written a very beautiful book, *Escape from Freedom*. The name is very significant: *Escape from Freedom*. He is right—everyone is escaping from freedom. For example, love is a freedom but marriage is not. Once you are in love, sooner or later the mind will try to escape from freedom and move into marriage. Love is unchartered, unknown—no one knows where it may lead. And freedom is infinite—one becomes afraid. So you make a cage, draw boundaries, and live within them. Then you know where you are and where you are going. You have escaped from freedom.

We are escaping in every way. Why? Because freedom is such a total thing, so big, and we are so small that we cannot face it, we cannot live with it. If you are alone you have freedom, but when someone else is there, when you are in a crowd, the freedom is lost. That is why everybody is trying to escape from loneliness: no one wants to be alone and free. One must have company because company means less freedom and more slavery.

David Riesman has written a book, *The Lonely Crowd*, in which he talks about this phenomenon. Everyone escapes into a crowd because to feel the pangs of loneliness is to be afraid—afraid of oneself, afraid of living with oneself. Everyone has done the same thing, so it is a big crowd, and everyone in it is lonely.

A person who is not capable of living with himself cannot be capable of living with anyone else. One who is not capable of loving himself, enjoying his own company, will not be able to be in a deep communion with anyone else. If you are bored by yourself, you will create boredom in others. So the crowds are there, but they are lonely crowds.

This freedom that you are asking about is the greatest freedom: to choose one's life, to choose one's being, to choose one's self. One becomes afraid. It is better to surrender to someone, it is better to let someone makes the choices for you—someone who is more expert, someone more knowledgeable, someone who can guide you. We go on escaping . . .

I have met many, many people who come to me and say, "I cannot do anything. I surrender to you—do something for me!" I am always surprised. If you cannot do anything, then how can you surrender? Surrender is a big thing. But people say, "I cannot do anything so I surrender," as if surrender were nothing, as if surrender meant not doing anything. How can you surrender if you have not chosen your life? If you think that you have not chosen anything, that you have just been thrown into life, can you say, "I have surrendered?" Who are you to surrender?

No! Surrender is the greatest act, a *total* act. Only a person who feels totally free can surrender, not a slave. How can a slave surrender? Only a responsible person can surrender. And if you can surrender, you can do anything.

This freedom must be understood deeply, not as a concept but as a situation in which we live. *We are free.* This very moment you can make an about-turn. There is no destiny that is forcing you in a particular direction, no past that is pushing you, no future that is pulling you—only you. You can turn around this very moment and change. You can be different, completely different. You can be a soul, not a body.

There are no degrees of freedom. And when I say that there are no degrees of freedom, no degrees of choice, I am also saying that there are no degrees of enlightenment.

You become enlightened suddenly. Just as there are degrees of slavery but no degrees of freedom, there are also degrees of ignorance but no degrees of knowing. Either you know or you do not know.

People come to me and ask, "Who is more enlightened, Buddha or Mahavir or Krishna or Christ?" As if there were degrees! People who write in the scriptures that there are degrees of enlightenment are stupid. "Buddha has attained this degree of enlightenment, Mahavir has attained that degree, someone else has gone beyond both . . ." There are no degrees of enlightenment!

Whoever evaporates, jumps. Enlightenment is a jump. Buddha's ignorance has degrees, Mahavir's ignorance has degrees, but the moment Vardhaman (the old name of Mahavir) or Siddhartha (the old name of Buddha) evaporate, their knowing has no degrees. Bliss penetrates the whole phenomenon of life.

Similarly, there are degrees of hate, but there are no degrees of love. There are degrees of anger, but there are no degrees of forgiveness—either you forgive or you don't. There are degrees of sin, but there are no degrees of virtue—there cannot be.

You are totally free to choose, infinitely free to choose. You can go on choosing repeatedly, birth after birth, for millennia. No one can tell you to change. You cannot change unless you yourself realize that it is enough. Buddha said, "It is enough. I have been, now I am going to be no more."

This is difficult to conceive of because logic feels that there must be degrees to everything. Reason says, "How can I say that I am free when there is bondage everywhere?" There is, but it is you who have created it.

Logic cannot conceive of it because logic is part of the mind and logic thinks in terms of rigid dualities. In logic, either there is white or there is black, either you are free or you are not free. In logic, there is no gray. But in life, gray is the only reality: white is one pole of gray and black is the other pole.

When I say that you are free, I am also saying that you are *free to be unfree*: you are free to be a slave. Your freedom is such that you can choose unfreedom also, because if you cannot choose to be unfree then your freedom is not total.

That is the dilemma. Ordinary logic will ask, "If man is free then why is he not free? If man is divine then why does he not feel divine? If man is bliss then why is man not in bliss?" But I say that man is unfree *because he is free*—he has chosen. Man can choose freedom and become free or man can go against himself, against his nature. That is what freedom implies. When you can go against your nature, when you can expand your consciousness or *not* expand your consciousness, you become free, responsible—or more damaging to yourself.

Animals are not free—not free in the sense that they are more unconscious. They live by instinct, they cannot choose. They have a fixed nature; they have to follow it.

Man has no fixed nature—there is no such thing as "man's nature." Man has freedom. He can fall, he can rise: he can go lower than the animals or higher than the angels. He has no fixed nature.

The more conscious you become, the less there is that binds you. The more responsible you become, the more dangers there are. Dangerous changes will be there, and you will not escape them unless you become totally aware. But it is good to pass through them rather than to try to escape because these dangers will help you to be more aware. Escape will only create unconsciousness, unawareness, lethargy and sleep.

Does the soul leave the body when you die? Where does it go?

This whole way of thinking—that something remains and something leaves—is fallacious. The gross body that we know is just a seed, the outer mask. There are also subtle bodies which continue to surround your soul even when it is leaving. These bodies are also part of you.

The body that is with me now is part of the universe, but because we conceive of our self as *ours*, it becomes a problem: where does my body end?

If you go into it deeply, you will see that the whole universe is part of you, part of your body. For example, if the sun were to cease this very moment, your body could not continue to exist. It could not exist if there were no oceans, it could not exist if there were no atmosphere. Your body is just a part, a constantly changing part, of the universe. When the sun rises, something rises in you. When the sun sets, something sets in you. When there is a moon, you are different. When there is no moon, you are different. Your body is in a constant, dynamic relationship with the whole.

Wherever you are, *whatever* state you are in, you will still be in a body. If your body is taken by the universe then the universe will give you another body—unless you consciously become the whole universe. Then there is no need for a body, because the universe itself has no body.

Individuals are bound to have bodies. But where does your body end and where does it begin? It is a problem, a multi-dimensional problem. Your body could not exist if your father's body had not been in existence. Your body is part of a long series, of an eternal series. Your body exists in the trees, in the sea, in everything. It is a small cosmos related to every part of the total.

Our language is very crude and limited, so when we say that the soul leaves the body, it gives a mistaken idea. The soul moves into the body of the universe, but the universe is constantly giving it another body. That body which you have left behind is still related to you, because the whole is related to you.

You are swimming in the sea. You have left part of the sea behind and gone ahead, but the part that has been left behind is still a part of the sea in which you are now swimming. The sea is one, and you are swimming in it just like the fish which is born of the sea and will dissolve into the sea. A fish is nothing but the sea itself, frozen somewhere, which will soon dissolve back into the sea again.

Our concept of coming into life and going out of life is primitive. You cannot go anywhere beyond this universe. Wherever you go, the universe behaves like a body to you. Your body is not only *your* body: it is a big community of many souls; you are only one of them. Every cell of the body has a soul, and each body has seventy million living soul cells.

Your body is a crowd of many many souls living in a big

city, and you are only *one* soul living in it. Each part of you is a soul in its own right: it can live and grow without you, it can love and reproduce without you; you are not needed. So when you have left the body, the body is still a living thing. The central soul has gone, but there are multi-millions of cells still living in the body which can ultimately develop, like you have, into a human being.

So it is a complex thing. But one thing is certain: nothing is dead; we are part of the ocean of life, we are aliveness.

It seems inconceivable to us because we go on seeing the universe from a particular point of view. That point is the disturbance. If that point dissolves and there is no ego to look from, then you cannot say that when you die you have gone somewhere. You have been. You will continue to be. Even though everything dissolves, nothing really dissolves; nothing ends. But that is possible only when there is no ego to say, "*This* is me."

We think that we are the center of the universe—just as mankind has always thought that the earth is the center of the universe. But even science has proven that this is not so. The fallacy that the sun goes around the earth is the same mental fallacy that we have about ourselves. It looks true even today, when we know it is not true. If we look, the sun seems to be circling the earth.

The same phenomenon happens deep down also. In religion also we are earthbound, egobound: everything seems to move around the ego. It is a fallacious idea; the reality is that you are going round the universe. You are part of it; you cannot be otherwise.

Whatever you think from an egocentric point of view will be wrong. For me, right and wrong have different connotations: for me, anything that has ego at the center is wrong and anything that has no-ego at the center is right. And unless you become one with the universe, unless the ego dissolves, you cannot have the right vision.

ELEVEN

Remaining Closed to the Lower: A Technique for Transformation

In this desperate spiritual situation, how can we get help from advanced souls in the astral place? How can we become open to the higher?

There is an old saying: "When the disciple is ready, the teacher appears." The disciple cannot find the teacher; it is impossible. Only the teacher can find the disciple. Only one who knows himself can know someone else. Then it is easy.

When you are ready, the whole universe begins to help you. There is no need to ask for any astral help, there is no need to go anywhere, help is always being given—a need is always fulfilled. But one has to be ready, one has to be in a state of mind where universal forces can help you. So it is not a positive search, because you cannot *seek* astral help; help depends on your receptivity, your readiness.

Higher forces are present everywhere, every moment. This very moment you are surrounded by both higher forces and lower forces, but you are receptive only to the lower.

You can either be open to higher forces or you can be open to lower forces; you cannot be open to both. The very mechanism of consciousness is such that if you are open to the lower you will be closed to the higher, and if you are open to the higher you will automatically become closed to the lower. We have only one opening, so it is your choice in which direction to move.

The first thing to be understood is how to be closed to lower forces and how to be open to higher forces. Higher forces are always there, but they cannot work unless you cooperate with them, unless you give yourself to them. The moment you are open to them the work begins—when the doors are open, the sun can come in. Your doors are closed. The sun is there, this very moment it is knocking on the door, but you are in darkness. You will remain in darkness not because the sun is not there but because your doors are closed. You have not invited the sun, you are not receptive to it. You are still not prepared to be a host—the invitation has not been sent.

How can one become closed to the lower forces and open to the higher forces? We are not even aware that we are open to the lower forces and yet we are in search of higher forces that can work on us . . .

For example, when someone loves you, you are always suspicious, always doubtful of it. Is the love true or not? Are you really loved or not? Is the person being authentic or deceptive? When someone is angry you never doubt whether he is really angry or just being deceptive, whether he is playing a role or is authentic. There is no doubt. It is always taken for granted that anger is authentic, but love is never taken for granted. You always believe the lower; you have a deep-rooted faith in the lower.

Remember, faith is the opening. Faith means trust, and whatever you believe in, you are open to. An untrusting mind is closed because it is afraid. But unless you trust you will remain closed.

The first thing to be considered is this: which do you believe in more easily, lower things or higher things? You believe in lower things without reasoning, without doubting, without thinking about it. You believe in the lower: the lower is your reality.

When Gurdjieff was just a child of nine, his dying father said to him, "I cannot give you anything except the one deep thing that I have experienced in my life. There is only one thing that I have gained that I can give you as my heritage: whenever someone is angry at you, don't react immediately. Wait for twenty-four hours and then reply."

Later on Gurdjieff was to say that this simple teaching transformed his whole life—he promised his dying father that this rule would be binding on him for his whole life. If someone insulted him, scolded him, or abused him, he would remain a witness to it with no immediate reaction—and not only outwardly but inwardly also. He would listen patiently to whatever was being said or done to him and then say, "I cannot react immediately. I will come back after twenty-four hours. This is a promise that I have given to my father. So I will come back after twenty-four hours and then I will react."

Obviously, he never reacted. He found himself coming back after twenty-four hours and saying, "At the moment I could not react because of my promise. Now, too, I cannot react." His whole life was changed by it, because the opening for the lower became closed. Twenty-four hours is too long a period to wait.

The mind opens only when there is a certain pressure— and then only for a moment. If you wait, the mind will close again. If you don't allow the pressure to affect you, then after twenty-four hours the situation will have become cold and dead. Only in a heated moment is the mind ready to react.

Because anger had become an impossibility, Gurdjieff tried this technique in other areas also. For example, sex. Whenever the urge was there, he would wait. After twenty-four hours there would be no urge: the mind would no longer be pulled by the lower force.

After practicing this for years, Gurdjieff suddenly became aware of other openings in his mind. Because energy has to flow, and the lower outlet was closed, it had to find a new outlet.

For example, passing by a church where a mass was taking place, he would just look at the people praying in silence and suddenly the door of his mind would open and he would become one with those who were praying; suddenly his mind would be open to something higher.

Then he became aware of another deep phenomenon. An ordinary person would pass by him while he was just walking along the street, and suddenly Gurdjieff would become aware that the person was not ordinary; he was a mystic. He would follow him. And he was one hundred percent correct every time!

Sufi mystics function very esoterically, so they have discovered secret ways of being recognized. Indian mystics want isolation, they want to be away from the crowd. They move to the forest, to the hills. But even if he moves to a monastery or the forest, people become aware of him, and before long he becomes known. Silence has its own message. It is its own message, conveying many things.

Sufis have tried another method. They do not go to a monastery, they do not go to a forest or to a lonely hill; rather, they become part of ordinary life. For example, a Sufi mystic may be just a cobbler. He will be so ordinary that no one will be able to recognize that he knows something, or he is something. But one who is open to higher forces will become aware of it.

This opening within Gurdjieff became the basis of his search for the miraculous. He followed—without any map, without any knowledge—and eventually came to India, to Egypt, and to Tibet. He went on and on—just feeling his way, not knowing where he was going—when suddenly he would feel that a particular footpath was good. He would follow it. Sometimes the footpath would end in front of a hut, and inside would be a mystic!

When you become open to the higher, things begin to happen in a very different way. But if you are only open to the lower then you have to grope in the dark for the higher. That groping is random, accidental. Sometimes you may come to know someone or something, but that is rare. Even if you stumble upon someone or something that could change and transform your life totally, you are not aware of it.

Even if you meet Buddha, you will not be aware that you are facing a Buddha. How can you be aware of it? You are not open to the higher, so even if you do meet a Buddha you will only be open to his lower possibilities. You will begin to find things to disturb you even in a Buddha: Why does Buddha eat like this? Why does he sleep like that? Why is he such and such? Your lower opening will give you things to think about that do not concern his Buddhahood at all, and the higher will be missed. The only thing that you will do is to look in the direction of the lower. It is such a long habit.

We believe in the lower forces, we are faithful to the lower, because only the door to the lower is open in us. If someone is condemning someone else we believe him totally; there is no need for evidence. That is why rumors become true: you can create an absolutely false rumor and then, because so many people believe it, it is possible that you yourself may begin to believe it. We are led by others. If so many people are saying something, it *must* be true.

The opening to the lower is habitual in us. Be aware when some lower force is pulling you. Be a witness to it. Don't allow your mind to be open to it. Everything that you are open to becomes deeply imprinted inside you and finally begins to work.

So be aware constantly, moment to moment. Even if something is right, true, but lower, don't be open to it. Even if you *know* someone is a thief, still I say: don't be open to it, because while you are focused on it, it is being imprinted within you. This habit of focusing in the lower is not good because it becomes a hindrance to the opening of the higher.

Buddha has said, "Don't believe anything that your ordinary mind thinks is believable." If I say that someone is a great saint, if I say that he is completely pure, your ordinary mind will hesitate to believe it. How can it be? He is in his body just as you are—how can he be pure? The ego feels hurt, so you try to rationalize it in every way. You cannot conceive of someone who is purer than you are, so you try to disbelieve it. But if you cannot conceive of someone's being purer than you, you will not be able to grow toward greater purity; then there will be no possibility of growth.

A Christian mystic, Tertullian, has said, "I believe in God, because only then I can grow." For Tertullian, God is not a question of fact or fiction but of inner growth.

For example, Nietzsche could have grown to be a Buddha. Such a great potential, such a great genius, such a vast possibility! But he did not grow to be a Buddha; rather, he grew to be a madman. When he said, "God is dead," it was not a statement about God; it became a closing to the higher for him. If there is no God, then there is no possibility beyond "this." Then, you cannot grow toward God.

You do not believe so easily that someone can be pure. A Buddha is so pure that you cannot believe it—even Buddha's own father could not believe it. When news reached him that his son had become enlightened, he is reported to have said, "I know him well—he is my son, my blood and bones. I know him better than you. He is not what you say."

After twelve years of wandering, Buddha returned to his home town. Thousands and thousands of individuals had become his disciples: he had become an inner light to them. But his father was totally unaware of the whole thing, and when he came to see him he was very angry. He was angry because Buddha was his only son—he had been his only hope—and he had deserted him in his old age. So when Buddha stood before him he said, "I still forbid you to do what you are doing. I am your father! I love you so much that whatever you have done I can forget—my doors are still open—but leave all this nonsense! I cannot bear to see my son begging in the streets."

For him, Buddha was just a beggar—in modern language, just a hippie—a rebel. Buddha stood there silently. Finally his father began to be aware that he had not replied. His father said, "I know why you have no reply. You have no courage."

Buddha laughed. He said, "Who are you talking to? The son that left your house is no more. I am a completely different person."

The father became even more angry—obviously. He said, "Are you trying to tell me that I don't know who you are? I have given birth to you!"

Buddha said, "You have given birth to me, but I do not belong to you, I am not your possession. You were just a passage. I am grateful, but don't say that you know me. You don't even know yourself so how can you know me?"

The father went on talking in the same way. He was not open to the higher being that Buddha had become, he was not open to the reality that was before him but only to the memory of Siddhartha, his son. A higher force was open to him, but he was open only to the lower. He was behaving like a father with his past memories—not even seeing the reality that was before him.

The whole thing depends on you. Buddha is not the monopoly of any age or any period; Buddha's power is always there, everywhere. One has only to be open.

The first thing to do is to be closed to the lower. Whenever your mind opens to the lower, just by sheer force of habit, remember continuously to be a witness to it and it will stop, it will close. Don't waste energy in the lower. Then you will not be dissipating energy, you will be accumulating energy, and the accumulated energy will help to throw open the door to the higher. Once you begin to feel the higher possibilities that exist, there is not even any need to think of the lower. The lower has disappeared: you have entered a different world, a different dimension, a new existence. And then you begin to receive help from advanced souls.

YOU ASK: *In this desperate spiritual situation, can we get help from advanced souls in the astral world?*

You can get help this very moment! The help is always there, but your eyes are closed. And not only are your eyes closed, you are emphatically in favor of their remaining closed. If someone tries to open your eyes, you use every argument against it. You say, "This is natural—darkness, sin, and evil are natural things."

For example: Freud brought about a great revolution. He did a great service in making humanity aware that regardless of what a man's potential is, ninety percent of his activity, his behavior, his thinking, is sexual. It was a great step, but because our mind is open only to the lower, the whole revolution went wrong. So when Freud said that the whole of human life, as it is, seems to be sex-centered, every religion fought against him.

It was a losing battle, because he was pointing out a fact. But now we are using that fact in a very wrong way. Now we say, "Yes, man is sex-oriented, sex-centered, but that is his nature—it has to be so." So not only ninety percent of human life is accepted as being sex-centered, the remaining ten percent is added to it.

These are the two lower possibilities: either one begins to fight sex and in the fighting the energy becomes perverted and goes astray, or one becomes a prey to one's own instincts and begins to flow toward sex with no possibility of any transformation.

Buddha and Mahavir and Jesus were trying to transform sex energy. Remember, to *transform* it, not to suppress it. But those who were open only to the lower and not to the higher heard it as suppression not transformation. Then the lower mind began to suppress, and perversion was the outcome—a Freud *had* to be born in order to bring man out of it. He had to emphasize that sex is natural: it should not be suppressed but accepted. Then, again, people began to move to the opposite extreme.

The lower mind moves to the other extreme very easily, because the lower opening only functions in two ways: suppression or indulgence. They appear to be polar opposites, but they are not. They help each other very mysteriously, like friends in a deep conspiracy. If you indulge too much then you will be pulled automatically toward the so-called opposite, suppression—and vice versa. Then the third possibility will remain closed to you—that of transforming the energy.

Both of these extremes are horizontal; and a transformation of the energy, the third possibility, is vertical. If you neither suppress nor indulge, the energy will not be able to move on the horizontal plane; it will begin to move vertically. That vertical movement is transformation. That vertical movement opens you to the higher forces.

When I say be closed to the lower forces, I don't mean fight them, I mean be aware. If you begin to fight you will remain in the lower and become perverted, which is even worse. Then you are not even natural; you become obsessed.

If someone is angry at you, remain closed; don't react. I don't mean fight against what you are feeling. I mean just be aware, wait; consider the whole situation and analyze it impartially; take every point of view. If someone is angry at you, first begin by considering whether he is right or not. If he is right, then be grateful to him. If you analyze very impartially and he is wrong, then there is no need to react because that will be his problem; you will not be part of it at all.

This is a very deep psychological insight: that if someone is abusing you, you begin to react only if you unconsciously feel that he is right. If you feel that he is absolutely wrong then you can laugh. If someone comes to you and says, "You are impotent," you will become furious only if you feel some sort of impotence somewhere, otherwise not. Only if what is being said hits something hidden within you is there a reaction. So analyze the whole thing, and if he is right then be thankful to him.

Modern psychology says that man's mind is divided into two parts: the minor part is conscious and the major part is unconscious. I may not be aware of my unconscious, but everyone who comes in contact with me will begin to be aware of it because it is expressed in my behavior, my gestures, my language. The unconscious is expressed in everything I do.

This becomes a problem, a deep problem. You are not

aware of your deeper attitudes, your deeper longings, your deeper suppressions, but others become aware of them. So learn to analyze what is happening. If someone is angry at you, analyze the situation. Maybe he is right. Then you will become aware of a part of your unconscious that you were unaware of before. Or he can be partially right and partially wrong—this is the third alternative. If he is partially right then be partially grateful and don't be bothered about where he is wrong. If he is totally wrong, then the statement is not about you; it is his problem.

When I say don't be open to the lower, I don't mean suppression, I mean analysis, observation, awareness, consciousness. If you suppress, then you will never be able to be open to the higher. A suppressed mind is deeply rooted in the lower because whatever you suppress you have to suppress continuously. If someone is suppressing sex, he cannot take a holiday from suppression. One moment's holiday, and the snake becomes alive again, with much vigor and vitality. With suppression, nothing dies. On the contrary, a thing that has been suppressed becomes more alive.

Be clear about the distinction between suppression and not being open to the lower. Remain closed to the lower. You have to begin from there because, as it is right now, your state of mind is open only to the lower. There are many people who try to open their minds to the higher without first closing the lower door. Then they create unnecessary tension and conflict in themselves, because unless the lower is closed, the higher cannot open; it is impossible.

First make every conscious effort to close the lower and then, without any effort on your part, you will sometimes begin to be aware of a different dimension. Just sitting under a tree, you will be transported to a different world.

You must have seen pictures of Buddha sitting under a tree. Have you ever thought about what he is doing? He is doing nothing; he is waiting. The lower has been closed, the accumulated energy is there, and now he is waiting for the right moment when the energy is such that it forces the higher to open. Many of the old meditation techniques are concerned only with this.

Buddha has mentioned many things to do in order to close the lower, but the basic technique is what he calls right-mindfulness, *samyak smriti*. That is the same thing that I have been talking about: awareness, alertness, observation, analysis. Buddha's own word is "right-mindfulness." He says, "When you are angry, remember that you are angry. Be mindful. Be conscious of the act." And this is an inner alchemical truth: that if you are mindful, you cannot be angry. You can either be angry or you can be mindful. You cannot be angry consciously because unconsciousness is the basic requirement for anger to happen: you can be angry only if you are unaware.

If you close the lower, the higher opens. And with the opening of the higher, you will be in contact with many phenomena. One will be what you have asked about: a deep communion with advanced souls. Nothing in existence is ever lost. Buddha is always there, Jesus is always there—nothing is lost. So for one who is open to the higher, Jesus is not a historical figure; he is still there. Twenty centuries evaporate and you are in contact with a living presence.

Buddha is still here—nothing is lost, nothing *can* be lost. Buddha, Mahavir, or Krishna are not just names and bodily forms, they became Buddha, Krishna, and Mahavir because they realized the formless. Now they are formless, they are eternal, so you can be with them at any moment; only an opening toward the higher is needed, because then time disappears. Both space and time are phenomena of the lower opening.

Scientists have said that this world consists of space and time. Einstein has made it only one: he says that time is a fourth dimension of space. He calls it spatio-time—this world is nothing but spatio-time. But when you are open to the higher you move into a non-temporal, non-spatial world. There is no time, no space.

When you are open to it, a totally different world is revealed to you. You are not only in contact with the higher but in deep communion with it. Then you are not. With the higher, you dissolve; only with the lower can *you* be.

That is why you insist on remaining with the lower—because in the higher, you will not be. The very existence of the ego, the self, the I, belongs to the lower. When you are open to the higher, you are not. And then, when you are not, you are simply guided by higher forces: you become just an instrument.

When Mohammed was in deep meditation on Mount Hira, suddenly he heard a clear voice which said, "Read!"

Being completely illiterate, he said, "How can I read? I don't know how to read, I am illiterate."

Again the voice said, "Read!"—but more forcefully. Mohammed hesitated. He began to tremble in fear. How could he read? Then, when for the third time the voice said, "Read!" Mohammed was standing on the boundary line between the lower and the higher. He knew very well that as far as the lower was concerned, he could not read. But the voice was from another realm. It persisted: "Read!" He opened his eyes and saw that he was in a different world. He could read. He could see.

This continued for years. The Koran was not delivered to Mohammed in one day, it kept on being delivered to him throughout his whole life. Mohammed had been an ordinary man before, absolutely ordinary. Suddenly he became different.

That is why Mohammed never said, "I am an enlightened one. I am a Buddha." Never. He never said, "I am the son of God," as Jesus did. He would only say, "I am an ordinary man—just a servant, just a messenger between two worlds." He was a simple, innocent man. That is why the lower closed and the higher opened. He was not making any effort for the higher to open, it just opened.

The first time it happened he became so afraid that he would not tell anyone. When he came home, he was in a high fever. It was so strange! how could he read? And what he had seen was so different, it was not of this world. He himself could not believe it—everything had turned upside down. He remained in the fever for three days and prayed. Then, very hesitantly, he confided to his wife what had happened. "I have been to a different world," he said. "But don't tell anyone or they will think me mad."

From that day on, Mohammed was guided not by his ego but by forces beyond him: he became just an instrument.

When the higher opens, everything turns upside down. Your logic will not apply, your reason will not apply. Whatever you have known becomes irrelevant; whatever you are becomes irrelevant.

YOU ASK: *How can we be open to the higher?*

It is possible by closing the lower opening. And it is essential for the survival of the human race that this happens.

It has always been so. The human race has survived only because of contact with the higher. You can pick out twenty names from the history of mankind: Buddha, Jesus, Mahavir, Lao Tzu . . . twenty names, and you will not be able to conceive how humanity could have survived without them. Darwin may say that we have survived because of the struggle of the animal world. And he is right as far as surviving as animals is concerned. But as human beings we have survived because of the higher forces that have been penetrating us all the while.

Whenever there is a Buddha, the higher penetrates the lower; through him the whole of mankind comes in deep contact with something higher. Buddha becomes a vehicle, a passage, a bridge. There are many bridges; because of those bridges, man is not just an animal, he is something more.

If man survives only as an animal, that survival is meaningless. And that is what is happening everywhere, all over the world. Those who contemplate the situation are aware that our lives have become just a meaningless, absurd repetition of the trivial, going on and on and on. We are just occupied, we are not living.

Only those who are not aware at all can think that this is life. Only very mediocre minds can think that this is life. If you think that this is all then life *is* meaningless. It is meaningless because, as an animal, man cannot have any significance. Man is a growth, a going beyond animality.

Buddha says that life is a wonder, a benediction. Krishna can dance and sign and celebrate life. We are just sad—sitting and watching life pass by like a meaningless journey, going nowhere. A boredom, a repetitive boredom. But for Krishna life is a celebration, a dance, a flowering. Why? Because he is in contact with the higher. When you are in contact only with the lower, life is just a trivial, meaningless, repetitive routine.

The world is not going to end in some atomic explosion, but it may end because of this meaninglessness. Whenever I think about the end of the world, it is never murder which comes to my mind but suicide. If this meaninglessness goes on piling up, humanity may commit suicide. It may commit suicide through an atomic explosion, but it will still be committing suicide.

The higher is needed, always. It is the only saving force. But we are more and more closed to it, we have denied it completely. And this is strange: that the same thinkers who have denied the higher now say that life is meaningless. If you show them any meaning they deny it. If you tell them that meditation can lead you to find meaning in life they say, "How? It cannot be—meditation is just a fiction. Where is this meditation? Show us what it is." They ask for scientific proof, they say, "We will experiment." Now they are trying to experiment with meditation scientifically. What are their conclusions? Their conclusions are basically these: that when someone is in deep meditation, he is nowhere but in deep, dreamless sleep. The mind waves are the same: when someone is in deep sleep, the mind produces alpha waves—these can be recorded now—and if someone is in deep meditation, the same alpha waves appear. So meditation is nothing but a deep sleep.

To outward appearances, that is right. You cannot deny it because there is scientific proof for it. If you go deep into meditation, the same waves appear in the mind as in dreamless sleep. So meditation is just dreamless sleep—the thing is finished!

It is not! Deep meditation is a stage beyond dreamless sleep. It is a waveless state where waves cease completely. When someone is moving into deep meditation he passes the state of deep sleep and then he goes beyond it. The recorder can record only up to the point where waves disappear; it cannot record what is happening in the state of no waves.

If the Buddha state is just like deep dreamless sleep, why waste time meditating for years and years? Why not take a tranquilizer? If the same alpha waves appear, then what is wrong with taking chemical help? It will be easier, more of a shortcut. The difference is that a person may take pills for years and yet he will not come to feel that life is meaningful. He may be able to sleep deeply, the same alpha waves will appear, but he will remain the same, in the same repetitive routine. He will not become wise, he will not become a Buddha. He will not be able to celebrate life, he will not be able to say, "I am happy that I was born, I am happy that I am." He will not be able to offer thanksgiving, gratitude, to existence.

Buddha is different, but scientists say they need scientific proof. Even if you could observe Buddha's mind, you would not be able to record what happens. When a Buddha is in deep sleep he is *aware*. But that awareness cannot be recorded because it is waveless. If you say that Buddha's state is just like deep sleep then you can still ask what the meaning of life is. Life remains meaningless.

Life becomes meaningful if you feel the existence of the divine, if there is a God. Meaning is possible only if the higher exists. Meaning always comes from the beyond; it cannot come from you. Only if you can go beyond does there seem to be a meaning of life.

But these same thinkers who want proof go on denying: "There is no God. There is no other state of consciousness." Then they ask what the meaning of life is!

Life is meaningless if you are only open to the lower. With the lower, there is only repetition of the same thing, again and again. With the higher, there is no repetition. There is eternal freshness, eternal virginity. Every moment is eternity itself. Then there is meaning in life, then your life becomes significant.

This contact with the higher is deeply needed for humanity to survive as humanity. Otherwise humanity can only survive as a species of animal—different of course, but not unique.

This has become the problem. We are struggling like animals: our politics, our nations, our races, our religions are all animalistic. When we say "nation," it is nothing but the greed for territory. When we say "race," it is nothing but herd worship. We give good names, we give good labels, and hide much ugliness behind them.

What is politics all about? It is like something animals do. You can see the whole political structure, the same politics of any capital of the world, even in a group of baboons. There is a president, the chief; then there are subordinates and servants, there are lower castes and higher castes—everything.

The chief is the super baboon. No one else can come near him; he has his own personal space. Even when the group is moving the chief moves alone: a certain space is left around him. Those who cross his boundary do so at their own risk.

There is a whole pecking order. The higher baboon suppresses the lower and the lower cannot even rebel. This is the inner politics; it continues every moment. Whenever a new baboon tries to become a chief, there is fighting and violence. Then, once again, the pecking order is changed and reshuffled.

Then, too, there are many baboon groups in a forest, each

group with its own territory which no other group can enter or there will be violence, war. The same has happened with man. This is the boundary: China begins here and India ends here. The question of the boundary is a great problem and ultimately only force decides where the boundary will be. If you go into politics deeply and if you compare it with a baboon group or any other animal group, you will see absolute similarities. In politics, man is just like an animal.

Only with religiousness, only with a religious consciousness, do you become human for the first time. Otherwise, everything is animal-like.

With religion, you have to be open to the higher. That is what religious consciousness is: to be open to the higher and closed to the lower. That is why a religious man cannot belong to any country or to any religion. He can belong only to existence, because that is the higher possibility—where there are no boundaries and no politics, where only religion is needed.

If this higher possibility does not happen, politics will become suicidal. Until now we have survived in spite of politics because we had no means of total destruction. We have survived in spite of politics, in spite of continuous wars. Wars and wars. Our whole history is made up of wars and of baboon chiefs—you may call them Alexander or Hitler, it makes no difference—fighting for territory, fighting for boundaries, fighting for ego power.

Man has survived in spite of this whole politics of war because there has been no total weapon. But now that we have total weapons we can destroy the whole world. And because of our animal tendencies, there seems to be no future for us. For the first time, religion has become the only means of survival: unless many many consciousnesses become open to the divine source, there is no future for us. We need Buddhas and Jesuses now more than ever.

What can you do? You can do one thing: close the lower opening; it is the only essential thing. But what are the difficulties you are likely to face? Only one difficulty: your old habits.

Old habits become automatic. Someone is angry and the next thing you know, your anger is incited. It has become so automatic—as if someone had pushed a button and the light went on. It is just like pushing a button. You need not do anything about it, anger comes so automatically.

Psychologists say that our mind is like a robot, an automatic machine—you need not be aware of it. Whatever you have learned you give to your robot and it will perform. Your mind is just like a computer. Once you have fed it, it will work. You can rest; you are not needed.

The robot is helpful as far as ordinary life is concerned, because without it you will not be able to do many things; it is a necessary help. But as far as higher things are concerned, the robot becomes a problem.

The robot knows when to be angry. You need not be aware when someone abuses you or looks at you in anger; the robot takes charge. It begins to throw poison into your blood, it makes you ready to jump in and fight. This is mechanical. You have to take charge of the robot—at least as far as the lower openings are concerned. It is good to let the robot drive, but don't allow it to love and to be angry.

Your robot is doing everything for you. It has done the same thing so many times that it has become an expert; you are not needed. When a husband and wife love each other it becomes a robotlike phenomenon; no awareness is needed. The robot goes on repeating things. Don't leave such subtle things to the control of the robot.

The robot is the only difficulty as far as spiritual progress is concerned. Take charge. Be conscious of things which have become automatic. Then, by and by, as you become more and more aware, the lower opening will be closed. And when the higher opens, you need not do anything more: then the higher begins to do everything through you.

You have to do something with the lower. With the higher there is only a surrendering—you are not. When we say "Bhagwan, Buddha," it only means that now Buddha is no longer Gautama Siddhartha—Siddhartha, the person, has dissolved—the higher has taken charge.

Even people who don't believe in God, who say there is no Bhagwan, no God as the creator, still call Mahavir "Bhagwan" for this reason: because they cannot call him by his old name. The person, Vardhaman, has dissolved completely. Now there is no ego functioning, now it is not Vardhaman who is alive; it is the beyond. Now the beyond has entered, the infinite has come within, and everything happens according to the infinite. Once you are open to the higher, you have dissolved: you are not, and the higher is. Then the miracle happens.

A Mohammed fighting becomes a problem for us. How can one who has become a higher being fight? But it is not a question of Mohammed's decision. Mohammed is no more; the divine has taken charge. Now it is the higher which is acting, and wherever it leads, Mohammed follows like a shadow. If the higher leads him into war, Mohammed goes willingly.

That is why Krishna is trying to convince Arjuna to surrender. "Surrender to me," he says, "and there will be no problem for you. Then I will take charge—I will fight through you."

But then, you are not. The whole struggle in the *Gita* between Arjuna and Krishna is due to Arjuna trying to remain himself: he wants to decide for himself whether to fight or not. Closed to the higher, he wants to decide according to the lower. He is resisting opening up to the higher and Krishna is insisting, "Close the lower and surrender to the higher. Then no decision will be needed on your part; then the higher will decide. Surrender to it."

Close the lower first and then, whenever you feel the higher, surrender to the higher. Whenever you feel the higher, have faith in it. Whenever you feel the lower, don't believe it, don't trust it; remain closed to it. Then you yourself will become a bridge to the higher.

T W E L V E

A Personal Seeking, An Individual Quest

Does God exist?

Something about right inquiry . . . Before you ask something, it will be good to know what is meant by right questioning. Every question is not a right inquiry, because as far as the inner dimension is concerned you can ask many, many questions that appear to be meaningful but are not; they are nonsense.

Metaphysical questions are meaningless as far as inner inquiry is concerned. Intellectual questions are meaningless. Intellect will not lead you inward, because even if you do get the right answer it will not be of any use. Intellect is an instrument, a bridge to all that exists outside; it has no door to the inner. So the moment you begin to ask intellectually, you can go on asking for many lives and collect many answers, but still you will not be connected to the inner world.

You can know many things about yourself, but to know something about yourself is not to know *you*. The "about" goes round and round on the periphery and the center remains untouched. You can go on in a vicious circle of questions and answers, and every answer will create more questions, then more answers, and then more questions. You remain on the periphery, asking and being answered, gathering much knowledge about the self without knowing the self.

How to ask something which can be meaningful—not simply intellectually but existentially, not just for verbal knowing but authentic living? There are a few things which have to be remembered.

One: whatever you ask, never ask a ready-made question, never ask a stereotyped question. Ask something that is immediately concerned with you, something that is meaningful to you, that carries some transforming message for you. Ask that question upon which your life depends.

Don't ask bookish questions, don't ask borrowed questions. And don't carry any question over from the past because that will be your memory, not you. If you ask a borrowed question you can never come to an authentic answer. Even if the answer is given, it will not be caught by you and you will not be caught by it. A borrowed question is meaningless. Ask something that *you* want to ask. When I say "you," I mean the you that you are this very moment, that is here and now, that is immediate. When you ask something that is immediate, that is here and now, it becomes existential: it is not concerned with memory but with your being.

Two: don't ask anything that once answered will not change you in any way. For example, someone can ask whether there is a God: "Does God exist?" Ask such a question only if the answer will change you: so that if there is a God then you will be one type of person and if there is no God you will be a different person. But if it will not cause any change in you to know whether God is or is not, then the question is meaningless. It is just curiosity, not inquiry. So remember, ask whatever you are really concerned about. Only then will the answer be meaningful for you. "Meaningful" in the sense that you are going to be different with a different answer. Are you really concerned about the existence of God? Will it make a vast difference to you if there is a God? Will you be a different type of being? And if there is no God, will your whole life begin to have such a different shape that you cannot be the same?

As I see it, whether God exists or not, people remain the same. They are interested only for the sake of peripheral knowledge. They are not really concerned; the question is not existential.

Immediately, here and now, spontaneously, let a question arise in you. Don't carry something from the past, don't carry something that comes from others, don't carry something that comes from the scriptures. Let it come from you. And even if nothing comes, that is better. If no question comes and you feel a deep emptiness, that is good. That emptiness is authentic, it is yours. Even in that emptiness much can happen.

If you ask in this way, from your deeper being, the very questioning becomes a process of meditation. And sometimes it happens that your question itself becomes the answer. The greater the depth it is coming from, the nearer it is to the answer. If you can ask from the very center of your being then there will be no need for any answer; the very question will become the answer. That is why I say that it becomes a process of meditation. If you can ask a question in such a way that you are totally involved in it and nothing remains outside the question, you have become the question. Then, no answer is needed. This very fact of *totally being* the question will become the answer.

An answer is needed from the outside only because your questioning is not deep. What I am saying is true as far as the inner search is concerned. In science, or with any outward inquiry, it will not be so. There a question will remain a question and an answer will have to be sought. But as far as the inner being is concerned, the question itself can become the answer, your quest itself can become the end.

In the inner search, means and ends are not two separate things. Means themselves are the end. Rightly pursued, the beginning is the end, the quest is the realization. But then the question must be total, authentic. You must be deeply committed to your question, it must not be just a peripheral curiosity.

So now, relax. And when I say "relax," I mean to relax your past, relax borrowed questions, relax your mind so that your being can emerge. Then this questioning will become a meditative process. Then anything that comes to your mind, don't hesitate to ask.

Why is there so much frustration in the world?

Because there is so much expectation. Expect, and there will be frustration. Don't expect, and there will be no frustration. Frustration is a by-product: the more you expect, the more you create your own frustration. So frustration is not really the problem; it is the result. *Expectation* is the problem.

Frustration is just a shadow which follows expectation. If you don't expect even for a single moment, if you are in a state of mind where there is no expectation, then it is simple. You ask a question and the answer comes; there is a fulfillment. But if you ask with any expectations you will be frustrated by the answer.

Everything we do, we do with expectations. If I love someone, an expectation enters without my even knowing it. I begin to expect love in return. I have not yet loved, I have not grown into love yet, but the expectation has come and now it will destroy the whole thing. Love creates more frustration than anything else in the world because, with love, you are in a utopia of expectation. You have not even been on the journey yet and already you have begun to think of the return home.

The more you expect love, the more difficult it will be for love to flow back to you. If you expect love from someone the other will feel it as bondage; it will be a duty for him, something which he has to do. And when love is a duty it cannot fulfill anyone because love as a duty is dead.

Love can only be play, not a duty. Love is freedom, and duty is bondage, a heavy burden that one has to carry. And when you have to carry something, the beauty of it is lost. The freshness, the poetry, everything is lost, and the other will immediately feel that it is only something dead which has been given. Love with expectation and you have killed love. It is abortive: your love will be a dead child. Then there will be frustration.

Love as play not as bargain, not because there is something you want to get out of it. Rather, love the other as an end in itself. Thank God that you have loved and forget about whether it is returned or not. Don't make a bargain out of it and you will never be frustrated; your life will become filled with love. Once love has flowered in its totality there will be bliss, there will be ecstasy.

I use love only as an example. The same law applies to everything. There is so much frustration in the world that it is difficult to find someone who is *not* frustrated. Even your so-called saints are frustrated: frustrated because of their disciples, frustrated because they begin to have expectations about them that they should do this and not do that; they should be like this and not be like that. Then frustration is bound to come, it *has* come.

Your so-called workers are all frustrated because they have expectations. Whatever their ideal is, society must conform to it; whatever their utopia is, everyone must follow it. They expect too much. They think that the whole world must be transformed immediately according to their ideals. But the world goes on in its own way, so they are frustrated.

It is very difficult to find a person who is not frustrated. And if you find such a person, know that he is a religious person. It makes no difference what the object, the cause, the source of frustration may be. One can be frustrated because of power, because of prestige, because of wealth. One can be frustrated because of love. One can even be frustrated because of God . . .

You want God to come to you. You begin to meditate and expectation comes in. I have seen people who meditate for fifteen minutes each day for seven days, and then they come to me and say, "I am meditating and I have still not realized the divine. The whole effort seems to be useless." They have devoted fifteen minutes to meditation for seven days and *still* God is nowhere to be seen. "I am still no nearer to God, so what should I do now?" Even in the search for the divine we have expectations.

Expectation is the poison. That's why there is frustration; it has to be so. Realize the falsity, the poisonousness of the expecting mind. By and by, if you can become aware of it, the expectations will drop and there will be no frustration.

So don't ask the question, "Why is there so much frustration in the world?" Ask "Why am I so frustrated?" Then the whole dimension changes. When someone wonders why the world is so frustrated, there is again an expectation that the world could be less frustrated. But whether the world is frustrated or not, *you* will remain frustrated.

The world is frustrated. That is a fact. Then you go and try to find out why *you* are frustrated. You will find that it is because of your expectations. That is the seed, the root cause. Throw it out!

Don't think about the world, think about yourself. You *are* the world and if you begin to be different the world begins to be different. A part of it, an intrinsic part, has begun to be different: the world has begun to change.

We are always concerned with changing the world. That is just an escape. I have always felt that people who are concerned with others' changing are really escaping from their own frustrations, their own conflicts, their own anxieties, their own anguish. They are focusing their minds on something else, they are occupying their minds with something else, because they cannot change themselves. It is easier to try to change the world than to change oneself.

Remember to find out the cause of your own frustrations. And the sooner you do so, the better. Situations differ, but the source of frustration is always the same: expectation.

I feel a lot of hate inside me. What can I do about it?

Doing will not help. You cannot do anything about it because the problem is very delicate. If you begin to do something about your hatefulness, that means that you will have begun to hate your hatefulness. The mechanism is very delicate. One can be angry toward one's anger and one can be hateful toward one's hatefulness, and you can fight it but you will not win because the disease has gone one step deeper.

Don't do anything. Just be aware of it. Whenever you feel hate, just be aware of it. Feel what this hatefulness is, feel the fact of it. Don't try to escape from it.

Even your doing can become an escape. If I am angry and I begin to do something about the anger, than I am not concerned with the anger itself but with doing something about it. My perception has changed: my awareness of the anger is no longer there but rather the effort to do something about it has taken its place. This is not good, this is not the way, because then the anger will be suppressed.

So if you feel hatred, anger, greed, or anything, don't try to do something right away, just be aware of it. First see the ugliness of it, see the poisonousness of it, see what it is. Once you see what hate is in its totality, it will drop by itself. Hatred can continue only if you have not known it in its totality.

It is just like a snake crossing your path. The moment you become aware that the snake is there, you jump. That jump is not something which you have to think about, decide about or choose to do; it happens. When you become aware of the snake, the jump happens. In the same way, when you become aware of your hate, the jump happens; no planning is needed.

The first thing to remember is this: don't condemn anything; rather, become more aware of the fact of it. Whenever it appears, be aware of it; meditate on it.

The second thing, which is even more subtle, is your thinking, I feel hatred inside me. I feel anger and greed and ego. This again is a very deceptive trick of the mind, a very cunning trick, because then, in a very subtle way, you have separated yourself from the hatred. You are saying, "I see hatred in me, I see greed in me. The greed is something which is *in* me, it is not me. I am not greed, I am not hatred, I am not anger. It is something accidental, something foreign that is inside me."

This is how the mind thinks and how language deceives us. Language says, "There is anger in me," but this is not the fact. When you are angry it is not that anger is in you . . . *you* are hate. There cannot be two entities there, only one. Either hate can be present or you can be present, but both cannot be present. If you are there then hate will dissolve; if hate is there then you are not there.

Move existentially not linguistically. Language creates many problems: because of the construction of the language we acquire a very unrealistic attitude toward things. For example, when you are angry, there is no I to whom anger is happening, there is only anger. You are dissolved in it; you are not.

Go into the problem existentially. When there is hate, become aware of whether you are there or only the hate is there. Then a very subtle change happens in your consciousness. Once you begin to be aware of whether "I am" or hate is, your consciousness begins to emerge. And the more conscious you become, the more the hatred will dissolve. Both cannot exist simultaneously. Hate is possible only when one is unconscious: not conscious, not mindful, not alert.

When hate has gone, anger has gone, violence has gone, and you think about it retrospectively it becomes part of your memory. Now you can divide yourself from it. You are separate from the anger and the anger is separate from you. Now it is part of your memory. This is how the linguistic fallacy I was talking about is supported by your experience.

You were angry a moment ago, now you are not—the anger has gone. You are separate from the anger: you are one thing, the anger is something different—the anger has become part of your memory. Now there are two things: the memory of your past experience of anger, and you. But in the act of anger itself, there was only one thing: *you* were anger. So whenever there is hate, feel it deeply. Be aware of it: you have *become* hate, you *are* hate. This awareness will change the whole thing. The day this awareness comes to you, hate will dissolve, because for you to coexist with hatred or anger or greed is not possible. Awareness means a *conscious* mind, and anger, hate, and greed are possible only in a very unconscious, sleepy state of mind.

Be more and more alert—and not retrospectively, because that is useless, it is a waste of energy. When anger is there, when hate is there, in that very moment, close your eyes and meditate on whether you are or only the anger is. Your first realization will be that only anger is. Where are you? You are not. Your whole energy has become anger, the whole of you has become hate.

Sometimes lovers feel that when love is there, they are not. To feel this in love is easy because love is gratifying, but to feel it in hate is difficult because hate is not gratifying. Lovers, deep lovers, have felt that it is not that they "love"— love is not an activity—rather, they have *become* love.

When you love someone you become love. When you hate someone you become hate. But if you just remain yourself, then you can neither love nor hate in the ordinary way. That is why we say that someone has "fallen in love." The phenomenon of love is a falling down, and "falling in love" means that you lose consciousness of yourself because of love. Lovers look mad to those who are not in love. They are! You cannot communicate with them, they are not in their senses. They *are not*, really; the whole energy has become love; they are identified with it completely. There is no witness to the phenomenon of love.

The same happens in hate. Love and hate are alike, because it is the same energy inverted. When you are in love you are madly attracted, when you are in hate you are madly repulsed. When you are in love, when you have become attracted to someone, you lose your center, your self, and someone else becomes the center. When you hate someone, the same thing happens: someone repulses you; you are not at the center, you lose consciousness of yourself, and someone else becomes the center.

Remember this—not retrospectively but in the very moment of the happening. When you feel that hate is there, close your eyes, forget the situation outside, and be conscious of what is happening inside you. The whole energy has become hate. If you watch it, then suddenly part of the energy will begin to transform itself into awareness. A pillar of consciousness will arise out of the chaos of hate or love or whatever. And the more the pillar arises, the more the chaos inside will drop and disappear. Then, when you feel that *you* are, you will notice that hate is no longer there: you become a self, a center; the other can no longer be the center which either attracts or repels.

This meditation has to be done at the very moment of the happening. Then you will be a different person altogether. Not that you will have conquered your hatred, not that you will have a controlled mind. Now you will be a consciousness, a light unto yourself. Because of this light, darkness will have become impossible. Now you are a conscious being. Hate has become impossible because hate needs your unconsciousness as its basic requirement.

This must be understood very distinctly and clearly. Hate needs your unconsciousness. That is the food for hate, that is where hate gets its strength. So don't do anything about hate, just do something about your consciousness. Become more conscious of your acts, of your thoughts, of your moods—of whatever happens.

A conscious being is neither hateful nor "loveful." That is why we have used different words in talking about Buddha. We could say that Buddha loves everyone, but then the word would carry the same meaning that we ordinarily associate with it. A Buddha cannot love you because he cannot hate you. He cannot be repulsed by you and he cannot be attracted by you either; in both cases, the other is the center. Buddha is not love but compassion, and the difference is very deep.

When you feel compassion, *you* remain the center; you can be neither repulsed nor attracted. It is a very neutral state. The other will feel very deeply that you love him, but . . .

If you come to a Buddha, you may feel that he loves you. That is your freedom. At any moment you can also feel that he hates you. That is also your freedom. It is your projection that he loves or hates. In fact, he neither loves nor hates; he remains himself, and the compassion flows.

See the difference? If you are not in this room, I cannot love you nor can I hate you. If I want to hate you I must have an object to hate, so if you are not here I will have to imagine that you are here. Love stops when the loved one is absent and hate stops when the enemy is not there. If they are absent, you make them present in your imagination.

Compassion means that even if there is no one there, Buddha will still be compassionate. It is not because of his imagination; it is his natural state. Just as a river flows, Buddha is compassionate. The other is not a part of it at all, the other is not the center, he himself remains the center.

When one becomes a center, when one becomes crystallized, there is neither repulsion nor attraction to anyone. This creates a deeper problem because it means that you cannot go beyond hate unless you go beyond love. Everyone wants to go beyond hate, but no one wants to go beyond love. But that creates an impossible situation for you because hate is a part of the one phenomenon of repulsion and attraction.

How can you just be in love, how can you be attracted to everything? We go on trying to love in many, many ways, but the only easy way is to hate one person and to love someone else. That is the easy way. You make one person your enemy and another person your friend. Then you can be at ease, you can love. You can be attracted to A and be repulsed by B. This is one way.

Another way, even more complicated, is to hate the same person that you love. This, too, we do. In the morning we love, in the afternoon we hate, and at night we love again. Every lover goes on continuously moving between hate and love, attraction and repulsion. Freud has said, and said very truly, that you have to hate the same person that you love—it cannot be otherwise.

This becomes more and more true as we get rid of all the scapegoats that we have had for our hatred. You could love your country and hate another country, you could love your religion and hate another religion because, if you love someone or something, you have to balance that love with hate. In the old days this was easy, the balance was there, but now the humanitarians, the utopians, have destroyed all our scapegoats. Soon the world may be so united that there will be only one nation, only one race. Then one thing will have to become the object of both love and hate.

This duality is a natural thing. If you love, then you have to hate. There are people who go on preaching: "Love the whole world!" But you cannot love the world unless you discover another world to hate. I don't think this planet Earth can become one until we discover enemies on some other planet. The moment we discover an enemy somewhere—and we are trying very hard to find one—then the whole world can become one.

When India is fighting Pakistan, there is no fighting within India; India becomes one. There is a very deep patriotic feeling for India because now that love balances the hatred toward Pakistan. But when there is no war, then Hindus fight Mohammedans, and *Brahmins* fight *Sudras*, one state fights another state, one party fights another party . . . and the thing goes on. But if there is an enemy somewhere, then the whole nation becomes one.

This whole earth cannot become one unless we have another planet to fight. Even a rumor would help. Linus Pauling, a great scientist, a Nobel laureate, once suggested that it would be good to create a world-wide rumor through the United Nations that Martians were about to attack the earth, and have scientists from all over the world support the rumor; then there would be no fighting on earth. And he is right. As man is, it would be a good thing. Lies may help. The truth has not helped yet.

With love, hate will be there and you will have to find some object to focus it on. So the more you love, the more you will be hateful. That is the price one has to pay. Remem-

ber this: either love and hate go together or neither of them is
there at all.

Hate will disappear not by your doing anything, but by
being more aware, more conscious, more alert. Become a conscious being and you will be at your center, and no one will be
able to take you away from your center. Right now, anyone
can do it. Some do it by love and some do it by hate, but
anyone can take you away from your center. You have no
center really, only a bogus center which is just waiting for
anyone to come and take you away from it.

Consciousness means centering, being continuously centered inside. Then both love and hate disappear. Only when
both disappear are you at peace.

And really, their symptoms are so alike. When you are in
deep hate you cannot sleep, and when you are in deep love
you cannot sleep. When you are in deep love your blood
pressure rises, and when you are in deep hate your blood pressure rises. All the symptoms are the same: you become tense.
When someone is in love he becomes tired, exhausted, and
bored by the ordinary things—just as in hate. Both are tensions, both are diseases.

When I say "disease," I am using the literal meaning of
the word: dis-ease. You cannot be at ease either in love or in
hate, you can only be at ease if there is nothing inside you,
neither love nor hate. Then you remain in yourself, alone in
your consciousness. You exist without anyone else, the other
has become irrelevant: you are centered.

Then, compassion will happen. It is a happening that follows once centering is there. Compassion is neither love nor
hate, it is neither attraction nor repulsion, it is a totally different dimension. It is just being yourself: moving according to
yourself, living according to yourself. Many may be attracted
to you, many may be repulsed by you, but these are just their
projections—it is their problem. You can laugh about it and
remain unconcerned.

*For the past ten years I've had a lot of
problems. I have a lot of anxiety. My mind*

seems to be going constantly. What can I do about it?

Why think about the past ten years? Why? That is the root cause of your problem.

What have you got from the past? Just memories and thoughts. You go on gathering more and more memories because every day your past becomes greater and greater. And the past is growing every day, because you go on accumulating thoughts, memories, experiences. Every day you have a bigger and bigger mind and less and less consciousness.

Mind means the accumulated past, and it goes on accumulating. What else can it do but go on repeating thoughts? What else is thinking but the repetition of the past again and again? Nothing new comes through. Thinking is never original; it cannot be, because you can only think in terms of the known. You *cannot* think about the unknown; you can only come to the unknown when you are not thinking.

Every day you give your mind more to think about. The mind goes on thinking—it is a very efficient mechanism. It can even make you go mad if you begin to think so fast that you cannot connect two thoughts. A madman is one whose thinking has gone to the very extreme: his thoughts overlap one another. You think linearly while a madman thinks along many lines simultaneously; his thinking is very complex.

If you go on collecting the past, your thinking will grow more and more. You may even begin to lose consciousness of yourself completely and then you will become an automaton, a computer, a thinking machine, a robot.

So what to do? Let the past be past. Don't carry it. Forget it. Remember only this moment. And the strange thing is that if you are really in this moment, you cannot think; it is impossible. Thinking is only possible in the past or the future, never in the present. Remain in the moment. Don't fall back into the past and don't jump ahead to the future. Remain in the moment, the moment that is occurring right now.

For example, I have been talking. I don't think that you

could have heard what I have been saying because your question must have remained working in the mind. You missed. And you can miss again this very moment. If you are really listening to me, your thought processes will cease. If the thought processes continue, you cannot be listening to me. If you are thinking about what I am saying—how to practice it— then you are again missing the present moment.

When you are eating, eat—don't do anything else. When you are listening, listen—don't do anything else. When you are walking, walk—don't do anything else. Remain in the present moment, remain with the activity, and soon you will realize that the past has drifted away and a new space has opened within you. In that space, there are no thoughts.

Live moment to moment. Die to the past and die to the future. Live here and now so that whatever you are doing becomes a meditation.

Meditation is an attitude not an activity, so whatever you do can become meditative. The so-called meditation that people go on doing is not meditation. It is the attitude of being-in-the-present which is the core, the central, the essential thing.

Do whatever you are doing—walking on the street, running, taking a bath, eating, going to sleep, lying on the bed, relaxing—and remain with the activity totally. With no past, no future, remain in the present. It will be difficult in the beginning—very difficult and very arduous—but by and by you will get the feel of it and then a new door will open, a new realm. Then the thought process will no longer be there.

By that I don't mean to say that you will become incapable of thinking; on the contrary, *only then* will you be capable of thinking. Thinking is a different thing from this mad rush of thoughts. This crowd of thoughts is not thinking at all. The thoughts go on and on, and you cannot do anything about them: you are just a victim, not a thinker. You suffer, you try not to think about them.

Try to stop a thought and you will see who is the master. Try to stop it. You cannot. The thought will rebel against your control and it will come back with a vengeance—with more force, with more skill and efficiency. Whatever you think about is not thinking, really, it is just a rush, a mad rush, a crowd, a traffic jam of thoughts—an inconsistent, useless, unnecessary holdover from the past.

So be aware. Don't waste the present anymore. Live in the present. Live in the meditative quality of the present.

The present moment is not really a part of time at all. Past is time, future is time, but the present is not time. Ordinarily, we divide time into three parts: past, present, and future. But in reality it is not so. The present is eternal, the present *is*. It is always here and now, an eternal now. In reality there is no past and there is no future. The past exists only in the memory and the future exists only in the imagination. Past and future belong to mind, not to existence. If you can understand this, you will see that time is mind and mind is time. Dissolve mind and there will be no more time, and vice versa.

That is why every religion insists that when you go deep down inside yourself *there is no time*: it is a timeless moment; that timelessness is here this very moment. You can miss it because of your wrong habit of accumulating the past, but it is there, and if you become aware of it, it can continue.

Be aware and, this very moment, the past drifts away, the future dissolves, and the present moment becomes alive. Live in it, exist in it, and then this mad rush of thoughts will not be there. You will become capable of thinking for the first time. This new thinking means more awareness, a more concentrated consciousness, a more focused light of your being. You become so aware that whenever a problem comes before you, your consciousness, your focused light of being, dissolves it. And when a problem is dissolved, you know the answer.

Your so-called thinking is more akin to anxiety than to thinking. In this so-called thinking that you do now, you have to grope for the answer—and groping can only be in the dark. Today you think you have solved something and tomorrow the same problem is there again, everything becomes confused again, and you go on groping and groping in the dark. That is why thinkers change their minds every day. That which was a truth yesterday is not a truth today and today's truth will not be the same again tomorrow. So everything is just approximately true—nothing is true, nothing is false—it can become false again any moment.

Buddha is true in a very different sense . . . *with no time-relationship.* Jesus is true non-temporally. Their truth cannot become non-truth because it is found not through thinking but through meditation, not through thoughts but through a process of no-thought. Remember this: *the process of no-thought,* which happens when you are in the present.

Bhagwan, when I love others it is a tension for me. Only my love toward you gives me a fulfillment, a freshness. Why is that?

This, too, can become a frustration at any moment because the other still remains the center. Whoever it is . . . the other must not be the center.

If you really feel intimate with me, then remember this: the other must not be the center. The moment your love is not centered on me you will be happy. If your love is centered on me that will only create problems. You will love me and you will find someone else to hate.

This is what happens. If you love your guru, then you will begin to hate and condemn all other gurus. If you love Ram then even Krishna becomes an enemy. If you love Jesus then how can you love Mohammed? You have to create an enemy.

If you love someone—even if you love me and you feel a freshness, a fulfillment—then, too, deep down, the other side will be there. Any moment it can erupt and become destructive. You must be fulfilled within yourself, because only then will there be no frustration. You will feel many things but they will be something separate from you. The center will remain.

If you can be with yourself totally, then even if I am not here, even if you cannot find me, even if you forget me completely, the fulfillment will remain, the freshness will remain. Then, when you are centered in your self, you can feel a subtle gratitude toward someone, but that will be a different thing.

Don't get attached. Don't think in terms of love, because the very term, as we know it, is bound up with its opposite. It seems difficult to understand. If you love me it seems inconceivable that you could hate me. But it is a common phenomenon. When someone is dreaming he cannot know that what he sees in the dream is just a dream. To him it is a reality; he cannot conceive of how it could be unreal. The same thing happens when someone is in love: he cannot conceive of how he could hate his loved one. But then, when he begins to hate the other, he cannot conceive of how he could have loved.

Those who love and then hate are not real lovers. But the mind goes on supplying reasons. If you love someone and you cannot conceive of how you could hate him or her, then the mind says that this is real love. Then, when you begin to hate the same person, the mind says that although you were a real lover, the other was not worth loving. First you find many reasons and causes and rationalizations for your love, then you find as many rationalizations for your hate.

I have seen this not only with one person but with many people. Sometimes it happens that someone loves me very deeply, then begins to hate me. And when someone loves deeply he can only hate deeply; there is no other way. When he loved me he could not conceive that hate was possible and now that he hates me he cannot conceive how that love was ever possible.

It is easy to move from love to hate, but it is very difficult to move from hate to love. There are many reasons for it. You cannot hate in the beginning; one has to love first. Love is a necessity in order to hate; you cannot hate directly without some love having been there. But then it is very difficult to put the broken mirror back together again. You can love again, but the hate which has preceded the renewed love casts a shadow on it. Something of the hate remains; part of it is carried over. The old fantasy of total love cannot be revived again.

If you love me, then you will feel hurt when I say this. Don't feel hurt. If you want to move toward self-realization, if you are trying to find a way toward the ultimate truth, then there will be many times when I will have to hurt you, when I will have to fight against your fallacies. I *know* that your love can become hate. And just as love has a freshness, hate also has a freshness, an aliveness.

But there is a love, which I call compassion, that can come to you. It can come to you only if *you* are at your center, no one else. Become more and more centered in yourself. Only if I can help you to do this will I have compassion. My compassion may hurt you sometimes, but that is needed.

So I say to you: anyone who is centered on someone else— whoever that someone else is—will become frustrated in the end. Become more and more free of others. That is why I allow you to come near me, that is my purpose in allowing you to be intimate with me—so that you can become yourself! If I can help you to come to that center in yourself where there is no love and no hate, only then will you be able to have an altogether different relationship with me. Then the quality of that relationship will not be of this world—neither hate nor love. Then you will not feel me as the other, you will feel me as yourself.

And not only with me . . . you will feel the whole world, the whole universe, as yourself. When one is centered in oneself, one becomes one with the whole universe.

But if you are centered in the other, then you will be in trouble—that is a natural consequence. And the natural law never allows any exception. It is absolute, mercilessly absolute.

APPENDIX

Between Death and Rebirth . . .

You have said that you remember your former life seven hundred years ago. Can you remember your name at that time and the occasion of your death? What I am interested in is what happened between your last life and your present life.

The question seems meaningful, but it is not. Life means that something is happening, and between two lives, there is nothing happening.

Between two lives there is a gap. If something is happening, then again it is another life. Nothing happens in the gap. You can remember it only as a gap, not filled by anything.

When we say that someone is alive we mean that something is happening in him. Life is the realm of happenings. Without a body, nothing happens: the body is the medium for things to happen. The moment you are beyond the body, or not in the body, nothing happens.

Then you can either be aware or unconscious: these are the two possibilities. If you are unconscious then you cannot remember. If you are conscious then you can remember. But the remembrance is only of the gap; there are no events.

Were you fully conscious of the gap between your last death and this birth?

Yes, I was fully conscious for those seven hundred years. I was fully conscious, but it was a consciousness of the gap, of the vacuum, of the emptiness, of nothing happening. Nothing can happen. "Happening" means being embodied. Only if you are in the body can anything happen.

Isn't it boring then to be without a body?

No, because the concept of boredom belongs to the realm of happenings. If something is happening continuously then you are bored. Boredom is also a repetitive happening. If you have to eat the same food every day then you are bored. But when nothing happens, boredom is impossible. You cannot be bored by nothing.

During those seven hundred years, was there any desire to be reborn?

In the gap between lives no desire is possible. Desire happens when you are dying. Even for a desire to happen you have to be alive and in the body. The desire happens when you are dying—and the last desire you have in one life becomes the first desire at the beginning of a new life. But in the gap itself, there is no desiring.

For example, when you go to sleep, be aware of your last thought: that will be your first thought in the morning. But there is no continuity of the thought in the gap, while you are asleep. Your last thought stops at this barrier, at this checkpoint, and it remains there. When you return to a waking state you have to pass through this same checkpoint again, over this same boundary, and your last thought at night will become your first thought in the morning.

The same thing happens when you are dying: the last desire that you have in one life will become the first desire at the beginning of the next life.

In the gap between two lives, everything that is part of life ceases—even time ceases. So when I say "seven hundred years," it is not my memory of the gap, it is only a reflection. In the gap itself time is not possible.

So many things are involved. Time is possible only when events are happening, otherwise you cannot create time. That is why, when many things have happened, *retrospectively* you feel that you have lived a long time. If nothing happens—if nothing happens for a whole day—then the day will seem very long. It seems very long because nothing has filled it; time has dragged on. But if you remember that same day, in retrospect it will seem very short because there were no events in it to make it look long.

On the other hand, if many things happen on a particular day, the day will seem very short. But if you remember that day, retrospectively, it will seem very long, because so many things happened.

Time is basically involved with events. If nothing is happening, you are not time-conscious—you cannot be; and space consciousness too is lost.

There is no dreaming between one life and the next. Dreaming is not possible because even dreaming needs a body. You cannot experience *anything* without a body—the body contains all the instruments of experiencing.

So if you are conscious between one life and another, you are only conscious of your consciousness. Nothing—no thought, no desire but the last desire—will have any effect on you. And the effect of your last desire is automatic, because to enter a body again was the last suggestion of your mind; nothing has to be done about it. If at the moment of death one dies fully conscious, with no desire, no thought, then rebirth becomes impossible.

If you go to sleep fully conscious, with no desire and no thought, then in the morning on awakening there will be no thought and no desire. In the same way the last thought that you have at the moment of death works like a seed, like a potential. Its working is automatic. Whenever there is an opportunity, a situation in which you can be reborn, you will be reborn. And if you have been conscious in your last life, then you will be conscious in this life also. Your birth will be a conscious birth; you will know what is happening.

Then that will be your last life. If this birth has been a conscious birth, then this death will be a conscious death. Then there can be no further birth possible. Once someone is born with full alertness, then that is his last birth. One more death will happen of course, but after that there will be no more births, no more deaths.

So when I say seven hundred years passed before this birth, it is just a reflection . . .

Selected Grove Press Paperbacks

E732   ALLEN, DONALD M. & BUTTERICK, GEORGE F., eds. / The Postmoderns: The New American Poetry Revised 1945–1960 / $9.95

E609   ALLEN, DONALD M. and TALLMAN, WARREN, eds. / Poetics of the New American Poetry / $3.95

B334   ANONYMOUS / My Secret Life / $3.95

B415   ARDEN, JOHN / Plays: One (Serjeant Musgrave's Dance, The Workhouse Donkey, Armstrong's Last Goodnight) / $4.95

E711   ARENDT, HANNAH / The Jew As Pariah: Jewish Identity and Politics in the Modern Age, ed. by Ron Feldman / $6.95

E611   ARRABAL, FERNANDO / Garden of Delights / $2.95

B439   ARSAN, EMMANUELLE / Emmanuelle / $2.95

E670   BARAKA, IMAMU AMIRI (LeRoi Jones) / The System of Dante's Hell, The Dead Lecturer and Tales / $4.95

E96   BECKETT, SAMUEL / Endgame / $2.45

E692   BECKETT, SAMUEL / I Can't Go On, I'll Go On: A Selection from Samuel Beckett's Work, ed. by Richard Seaver / $6.95

B78   BECKETT, SAMUEL / Three Novels: Molloy, Malone Dies and The Unnamable / $3.95

E33   BECKETT, SAMUEL / Waiting for Godot / $2.95

B411   BEHAN, BRENDAN / The Complete Plays (The Hostage, The Quare Fellow, Richard's Cork Leg, Three One Act Plays for Radio) / $4.95

E531   BERGMAN, INGMAR / Three Films by Ingmar Bergman (Through A Glass Darkly, Winter Light, The Silence) / $4.95

E331   BIELY, ANDREY / St. Petersburg / $6.95

E417   BIRCH, CYRIL and KEENE, DONALD, eds. / Anthology of Chinese Literature, Vol. I: From Early Times to the 14th Century / $8.95

E584   BIRCH, CYRIL, ed. / Anthology of Chinese Literature, Vol. II: From the 14th Century to the Present / $4.95

E368   BORGES, JORGE LUIS / Ficciones / $3.95

E472   BORGES, JORGE LUIS / A Personal Anthology / $3.95

B312   BRECHT, BERTOLT / The Caucasian Chalk Circle / $1.95

B414   BRECHT, BERTOLT / The Mother / $2.95

B108   BRECHT, BERTOLT / Mother Courage and Her Children / $1.95

E580   BRETON, ANDRE / Nadja / $3.95

B193   BULGAKOV, MIKHAIL / The Heart of a Dog / $2.95

B171	RECHY, JOHN / Numbers / $2.95
E710	REED, ISHMAEL and YOUNG, AL, eds. / Yardbird Lives! / $5.95
B112	ROBBE-GRILLET, ALAIN / For A New Novel: Essays on Fiction / $2.25
B69	ROBBE-GRILLET, ALAIN / Two Novels: Jealousy and In the Labyrinth / $4.95
E698	ROBBE-GRILLET, ALAIN / Topology of a Phantom City / $3.95
E759	ROBERTS, RANDY / Jack Dempsey: The Manassa Mauler / $6.95
E741	ROSSET, BARNEY, ed. / Evergreen Review Reader: 1962–1967 / $12.50
B207	RULFO, JUAN / Pedro Paramo / $1.95
B138	SADE, MARQUIS DE / The 120 Days of Sodom and Other Writings / $7.95
B323	SCHUTZ, WILLIAM C. / Joy: Expanding Human Awareness / $1.95
B313	SELBY, HUBERT, JR. / Last Exit to Brooklyn / $2.95
B363	SELBY, HUBERT, JR. / The Room / $1.95
B1	SINGH, KHUSHWANT / Train to Pakistan / $2.95
E618	SNOW, EDGAR / Red Star Over China / $5.95
E684	STOPPARD, TOM / Dirty Linen and New-Found-Land / $2.95
E703	STOPPARD, TOM / Every Good Boy Deserves Favor and Professional Foul: Two Plays / $3.95
B319	STOPPARD, TOM / Rosencrantz and Guildenstern Are Dead / $2.25
E231	SUZUKI, D. T. / Manual of Zen Buddhism / $3.95
E749	THELWELL, MICHAEL / The Harder They Come / $7.95
B452	TOOLE, JOHN KENNEDY / A Confederacy of Dunces / $3.50
B399	TRUFFAUT, FRANCOIS / Small Change / $1.95
B395	TRUFFAUT, FRANCOIS / The Story of Adele H / $2.45
E699	TURGENEV, IVAN / Virgin Soil / $3.95
E328	TUTUOLA, AMOS / The Palm-Wine Drinkard / $2.45
E84	WALEY, ARTHUR / The Way and Its Power: A Study of the Tao Te Ching and Its Place in Chinese Thought / $4.95
E579	WARNER, LANGDON / The Enduring Art of Japan / $4.95
B365	WARNER, SAMUEL J. / Self Realization and Self Defeat / $2.95
E219	WATTS, ALAN W. / The Spirit of Zen / $2.95
B106	YU, LI / Jou Pu Tuan / $1.95

GROVE PRESS, INC., 196 West Houston St., New York, N.Y. 10014